Praise for *The C*

"Approachable and charming, Kelden is every bit as serious and thoughtful as Traditional Witchcraft's most respected teachers, but with a youthful, down-to-earth delivery that both newcomers and old-timers will appreciate. Whether you are interested in building your own path as a Traditional Witch or you are simply curious about this increasingly prevalent flavor of the Craft, this is the book you need."

—Thorn Mooney, author of *Traditional Wicca*

"In *The Crooked Path*, Kelden teaches us how to harness the fundamental aspects of Traditional Witchcraft and mysticism. From roots and bones to moon workings and the Witches' Sabbath, this book is a treasure trove of valuable information and insight that no Traditional Witch should be without. Highly recommended."

—Devin Hunter, author of *The Witch's Book of Mysteries*

"*The Crooked Path* is the book we've all been waiting for. From basic tools to crossing the hedge, Kelden has included all the knowledge a newcomer to Traditional Witchcraft could possibly need. *The Crooked Path* is filled with historical folklore, rituals, and exercises that will strengthen your connection with your own practice. This book is a must-read for all who aspire to work with a realm beyond the physical and embrace their inner witch."

—Maggie Elram, co-creator of *The Traditional Witch's Deck*

"Kelden has conjured forth a comprehensive introduction that meets his intentions. This is a book that is down-to-earth, clear, earnest, and clever—some might say cunning. This is a book I will recommend to seekers of Traditional Craft as a way to explore and orient to a mysterious set of traditions and ways that are largely mysterious and otherworldly."

—Gede Parma, author of *Ecstatic Witchcraft*

"Kelden has succeeded in the challenging task of distilling the core elements and themes of traditional Craft into an approachable and moving system. These are practices of the common people, and *The Crooked Path* proves they can be deep and powerful without the need for inaccessible jargon. The work within is both timeless and beautifully relevant."

—David Salisbury, author of *The Deep Heart of Witchcraft*

"*The Crooked Path* is a concise, approachable, yet solidly concrete guide to Traditional Witchcraft for the modern practitioner. This lovely book blends practical insight with mythic inspiration and historical context—without the clutter of ego and overwrought occultism that plagues so many other books in the genre. Let Kelden be your guide to exploring and experiencing these mysteries, aiding you to find your own authentic Witch way with confidence."

—Laura Tempest Zakroff, author of *Weave the Liminal*

"Drawing from many sources, Kelden offers history as well as ritual and lore geared toward assisting the reader in embarking on an authentic journey to the Witches' Sabbath and the (re)discovery of our own magical power."

—Storm Faerywolf, author of *Forbidden Mysteries of Faery Witchcraft*

"Kelden's *The Crooked Path* offers a lively perspective of the principles and praxis of Traditional Witchcraft. Uniting historical information with simple and accessible instructions and recipes, *The Crooked Path* invites readers to tailor their Craft to the land on which they live. Kelden underscores his points with folklore from the Old World and the New, providing a book that is a valuable link in a chain that draws Traditional Witchcraft into the modern day."

—Nicholas Pearson, author of *Stones of the Goddess*

"Kelden is adroit at navigating a tradition that has as many different beliefs and practices as it has practitioners.... *The Crooked Path* is an excellent, thorough introduction to the complex practices of Traditional Witchcraft."

—*Foreword Reviews*

THE
CROOKED
PATH

About the Author

Kelden (Minnesota) has been practicing Traditional Witchcraft for more than a decade. In addition to being the co-creator of the Traditional Witch's Deck, his writing has appeared in *The Witch's Altar*, *The New Aradia: A Witch's Handbook to Magical Resistance*, and *Modern Witch* magazine. Furthermore, he authors a blog on the Patheos Pagan channel called *By Athame and Stang*. In his free time, Kelden enjoys reading, hiking, growing poisonous plants, and playing ukulele.

THE CROOKED PATH

An Introduction to Traditional Witchcraft

KELDEN

Foreword by GEMMA GARY

Llewellyn Publications
Woodbury, Minnesota

FIRST EDITION
Eighth Printing, 2024

Cover design by Shannon McKuhen
Interior illustrations by Llewellyn Art Department

Llewellyn Publications is a registered trademark of Llewellyn Worldwide Ltd.

Library of Congress Cataloging-in-Publication Data
Names: Kelden, author.
Title: The crooked path : an introduction to traditional witchcraft /
  Kelden.
Description: First edition. | Woodbury, Minnesota : Llewellyn Worldwide.
  Ltd, 2020. | Includes bibliographical references. | Summary: "A primer
  for readers new to the practice of Traditional Witchcraft, which is
  rooted in folklore and history. Shares hands-on tips and techniques for
  establishing a practice that is based on your own location and natural
  landscape. Explains how to work with the tools, rituals, and spells of
  Traditional Witchcraft and explores connecting to ancestors, familiar
  spirits, and deities"—Provided by publisher.
Identifiers: LCCN 2019037498 (print) | LCCN 2019037499 (ebook) | ISBN
  9780738762036 (paperback) | ISBN 9780738762081 (ebook)
Subjects: LCSH: Witchcraft.
Classification: LCC BF1566 .K455 2020 (print) | LCC BF1566 (ebook) | DDC
  133.4/3—dc23
LC record available at https://lccn.loc.gov/2019037498
LC ebook record available at https://lccn.loc.gov/2019037499

Llewellyn Worldwide Ltd. does not participate in, endorse, or have any authority or responsibility concerning private business transactions between our authors and the public.

All mail addressed to the author is forwarded but the publisher cannot, unless specifically instructed by the author, give out an address or phone number.

Any internet references contained in this work are current at publication time, but the publisher cannot guarantee that a specific location will continue to be maintained. Please refer to the publisher's website for links to authors' websites and other sources.

Llewellyn Publications
A Division of Llewellyn Worldwide Ltd.
2143 Wooddale Drive
Woodbury, MN 55125-2989
www.llewellyn.com

Printed in the United States of America

*To Veles, my soul-friend and
constant companion along this Crooked Path.*

Disclaimer

The information contained in this book derives from historical and folkloric sources, as well as from personal experience. It is in no way meant to replace qualified medical care, including that provided by mental health professionals. The author and publisher are not liable for any injury or ill effect caused by the application of information provided in this book. Do not ingest poisonous or unfamiliar plants, and take care when handling them. Please use your common sense when utilizing any of the practices discussed and consult the advice of a trained medical practitioner when necessary.

Acknowledgments

The book you are about to read simply would not have been possible to write if not for the wonderful people in my life. First and foremost, I'd like to thank my family—Mom, Dad, Breanna, and Colton. Family is everything to me, and the love that we share is the most powerful magic that I have ever experienced. Second, I'd like to thank my friends Diana, Maggie, Dana, Sara, and Marina, who have always had my back and supported my dreams. Additionally, I'd like to thank my fellow writers at Patheos Pagan, who continuously inspire me to be a better Witch and writer. I'd like to thank the team at Llewellyn Publications for believing in me and my vision for this book. I'd also like to thank Gemma Gary for graciously writing the foreword to this book. Finally, as always, I'd like to thank the Witch Father and Witch Mother, the spirits of my ancestors and those of the land, the Fair Folk, and my familiar spirit.

Contents

Exercises

From the Black Book

FOREWORD

The origins and lore of today's Witchcraft are a tangled thicket, and its traditions and variants a skein of many strands. In following our way back along the elder threads, we find the old Witch beliefs, giving rise to those considered "beyond the pale" and feared for their uncanny powers to curse (and sometimes to cure), powers long attributed to encounters and relationships with the Devil, familiar spirits, or some other envoy of the Otherworld. So too do we pick up the threads that lead us to the old-time "white witches," conjurors, and Cunning Folk of both rural and urban communities, whose Craft was one of operative magic, of divining and blessing or blasting, according to the needs and wants of a paying clientele.

Here might be perceived a heritage of sorts, for whilst some Cunning Folk drew their knowledge and power from apparent possession of magical texts, accounts tell of others dealing with familiars and having had encounters with spirits and otherworldly beings from whom they gained their ability to provide cures, perform divinations, and counter the ill influence of the malevolent Witch.

In Britain, this particular strand of Witchcraft reached its height in the nineteenth century, gradually fading and having all but disappeared by the 1930s. However, beneath this apparent decline, shifts and changes had long been afoot. The rise of clandestine initiatory fraternities, group occultism, and popular spiritualism through the eighteenth and nineteenth centuries may well have provided an environment and a confluence of ideas in which once-solitary practitioners of cunning traditions and Witchcraft evolved working lodge and coven structures in which to consolidate, nurture, and continue their artes and mysteries.

The first, and thereafter most prominent, such brand of coven Witchcraft to emerge into public consciousness was of course that promulgated by Gerald

Brosseau Gardner. Evidently, his was a vision of a Witchcraft for the masses, and so Gardner set about reworking and building upon the possibly fragmentary form of witchcraft into which he had been initiated in the 1930s. Drawing upon his interests in Romantic era Paganism, Freemasonry, and ceremonial occultism, Gardner was able to forge a beautiful and workable system of celebratory Pagan Witchcraft for the new Aquarian Age.

Other Craft traditions and recensions would however emerge, often at odds with Gardner and his innovations, claiming to represent pre-Gardnerian "Old Craft" approaches to Witchcraft. These typically emphasized operative cunning, less formalized ritual, and a gnostic mysticism drawing upon the virtues and hidden presences of the landscape, the spirit world, and folkloric practices. Thus was the Traditional Witchcraft movement born, seeing those claiming to represent elder traditions and those drawing inspiration from historical Witchcraft presenting alternative paths to Wicca.

Whilst, of course, Gardner's vision for the Craft has been phenomenally successful, serving admirably the needs of many called to its approach to the mysteries, there is undoubtedly a current resurgence in those expressions of Craft that are more magically operative in emphasis, rather than celebratory. There appears to be a great desire for a Craft that is rooted deeply in those lonely and numinous places of power within the land, in which potent virtues may be drawn forth, spirit allies enjoined, and the way crossed betwixt the worlds. Here too may the materia magica of plant, stone, and bone be sought in hedge, field, and forest and at the water's edge. It is with the aid of such spirit forces and nature-given tools that a great number of seekers unto the arte magical are now drawn to work the ways of the Witch's eye, of blessing and blasting, of exorcism and conjuration, and to craft amulet, charm, and talisman.

Whilst in the Old Craft the spirit forces and the whispering wisdom of the wild and lonely places are primary teachers, the guidance of one who has trod the round of the wise many times is invaluable. However, few have access to such a guide, and even fewer the opportunity to share the warmth and wisdom at the hearth of assembled company, coven, or clan. And so, it is books, wrought of dedication, insight, and experience and pointing the way to self-navigating the hooks and crooks of the Traditional Witch's path, that many turn to in search of true guidance.

The seeker will find such guidance within these very pages, for Kelden parts the thorny overgrowth at the stile and invites the would-be journeyman to traverse and explore the ways that lead to the heart of the Elder Craft. Herein are carefully mediated paths of inner workings to forge and temper; of power and its employment; of crafting and hallowing the tools of the arte where force, symbolism, and form unite; of Witch-rite and ceremony; and of the operative magics of wort cunning, charm crafting, and spell working. Here imparted too are ways unto the mysteries of familiar and fetch and the forging of a working relationship with the Old Ones, the spirit world, and the land.

As one whose Craft background arises from mixed streams, I welcome this book also for its refreshing absence of derision when discussing other forms of Craft. As Cecil Williamson once wrote, "Those who work witchcraft are on the whole a divided lot each calling stinking fish to the other groups' methods."[1] Such a trait has long plagued the post-revival Craft. Yet within Kelden's writing is recognition of the fact that all branches of the Craft are reaching forth in different directions, all from an old, gnarled, and twisted trunk, itself arising from tangled roots fathoms deep.

For those drawn to the many-fingered branch of Traditional Witchcraft and the living artes of Witch, wise woman, and cunning man, here unfolds the ever revealing, ever concealing, serpentine way of the Crooked Path.

—Gemma Gary
July 2019

---

1. Kerriann Gowdin, ed., *The Museum of Witchcraft: A Magical History* (Bodmin, UK: The Occult Art Company and the Friends of the Boscastle Museum of Witchcraft, 2011), 18.

INTRODUCTION

From a very young age, I had a natural curiosity about Witchcraft and magic. In fact, I can't actually remember a time when I wasn't wholeheartedly interested in Witches, ghosts, and faeries. I spent the majority of my childhood playing in the woods next to my house, collecting herbs, building faerie houses, and reading from books of spells. I felt most at home among the trees, befriended by the birds, the deer, and an assortment of spirits. It was in those woods that I first felt connected to a higher power or deity. But unlike the god I was taught about during my brief time spent in church, whoever this was didn't feel distant or disconnected from me. Instead, we would sing together under the moonlight and dance around the giant oak tree. When I'd have a bad day, I'd curl up on the ground and they'd hold me while I cried into the dirt. My world was an enchanted one, where every plant and stone had a spirit, the moon herself was a goddess, and magic flowed from my very fingertips.

When I was eleven years old, I discovered Wicca while searching the internet (still a relatively new innovation) for information on Witchcraft. Discovering that there were other people out there who identified as Witches was an incredibly validating experience for me. It meant that I wasn't as alone as I sometimes felt and that there was a reality to my beliefs—which were very different from those of everyone else I knew. From that point forward, my practice as a solitary, eclectic Wiccan took off. I was lucky to have supportive parents who bought me my first books on Wicca and Witchcraft, and I read whatever I could get my hands on. However, by the time I entered college, I felt something had changed—that I had reached a plateau in my path. The books I read felt increasingly redundant, and even the rituals I had performed countless times before seemed to become hollow and lifeless. At that point I decided to try reinvigorating my practice by researching the history of Witchcraft in more depth. I turned to the books written by the early pioneers of modern Witchcraft, including Gerald Gardner, Doreen Valiente, Janet and Stewart Farrar, and Alex and Maxine Sanders. Then I worked backward, using their references and bibliographies to find even older sources. During my studying, two things eventually became abundantly clear: one, that there was far more to Wicca than what was often presented in the popular, easily accessible books; and two, that despite my deepened love and respect for Wicca, it was no longer the right path for me.

It was while researching the history of Wicca that I discovered another path of Witchcraft, one that felt more like home to me. I had almost missed it entirely, a nearly hidden exit off the main road. I pushed through the thorny brambles and found myself on a new trail, one that was built into the living landscape around me. It was muddy, organic, and wild. The Craft of those who walked along this roadway was practiced in the garden and in the kitchen, in this world and the Otherworld. Its core beliefs hearkened back to my early years of fairytale Witches and magic, with familiar spirits, potions made from deadly plants, and spells whispered on the wind. The words and rituals were those from the heart, spoken and performed by the Witch in ecstasy while surrounded by the spirits. It was founded on the ancestral wisdom of the Witches who came before, enchanted by their stories, whether they be fact, fiction, or somewhere in between. It was a path that I found mysterious, fascinating, and inescapable. It was a crooked path called Traditional Witchcraft.

Now, nearly a decade later, I feel deeply rooted in my practice as a Traditional Witch. Over the years I have grown to be an avid researcher, writer, and presenter on the topic of Traditional Witchcraft, as well as the history and folklore of Witchcraft in general. I have published essays in various books, presented workshops, written a blog, and cocreated an oracle deck. It's an understatement to say that a lot has changed since I took my first steps onto the Crooked Path. Though, in reflecting upon the early days of my journey, I've come to realize that there was one thing lacking during that time—a quality book for the beginning Traditional Witch to help guide the way.

Why It's Important

As I started to look more into Traditional Witchcraft, I was quick to find a discrepancy between the amount of available resources dedicated to this path and those focused on Wicca. It hasn't been until the last decade or so that books on Traditional Witchcraft have started to be published with more frequency. Thus, there haven't been all that many books to choose from and even fewer that are written with the beginner in mind. In fact, the vast majority of Traditional Witchcraft books are geared toward those who already have some amount of prior knowledge and experience. Unfortunately, this can leave newcomers feeling confused due to a lack of explanation on essential topics. To make matters worse, some of these resources are completely unapproachable due to their use of overly complicated, dramatic language. Together, these factors have made it incredibly difficult for beginners to find a solid place to start their journey and have even turned some away completely.

A further problem that I've noticed in several books on Traditional Witchcraft is the ridiculous amount of material dedicated to trying to differentiate between it and Wicca. Most of this is due to the period of time in which those books were written, when Wicca was still the front and center of all things Witchcraft related. Therefore, differentiating between the two was more important, as people were less familiar with non-Wiccan forms of the Craft. Even today, discussions on how they relate to one another can be helpful. However, when every subject mentioned in the book contains a diatribe about how it's completely different from Wicca, the focus tends to get lost. Of course, this is also before taking into consideration the annoying habit of Wicca bashing, which is petty and consequently detracts from an author's credibility.

In writing *The Crooked Path: An Introduction to Traditional Witchcraft*, it was my goal to create the book I wish I would have had when first learning the ways of Traditional Witchcraft, a book that cuts through the pretenses and presents the material in a practical, down-to-earth manner. It's also been my goal to write a book on Traditional Witchcraft that discusses its relationship with Wicca in a fair and balanced way. Having spent considerable time as a researcher and a participating member of both paths, it's been my long-standing desire to dismantle stereotypes and misinformation while also working toward creating a better understanding of both Wicca and Traditional Witchcraft. My hope for this book is that it will provide you with all this and more, whether you're already a practicing Traditional Witch, a beginner, or just someone who is curious to know more about this particular branch of Witchcraft.

How to Use This Book

The Crooked Path: An Introduction to Traditional Witchcraft contains thirteen chapters, divided into five parts. The book is laid out as a metaphorical path, with each chapter taking you a step further on your journey. As you walk the winding road, you'll learn about the definition and history of Traditional Witchcraft, how to work with magic, how to travel into the Otherworld, and how to forge a deep connection with the natural world around you. In the final part of this book, you will take everything you've learned and put all the pieces together in order to establish your very own Traditional Witchcraft practice.

Along the way, you will find numerous exercises, rituals, and spells to engage your mind and get your hands dirty. If you don't already have a journal, I encourage you to start one so that you can write down your responses and reactions to these exercises. Additionally, throughout the book, you will discover sections entitled "From the Spirits of Lore" and "From the Black Book." The former will provide you with folkloric stories that are meant to highlight and add further context to topics being discussed. In the latter sections, you will find helpful recipes for various incenses, powders, ointments, waters, and offerings. Finally, please refer to the back of this book for a glossary of terms and a bibliography containing excellent books for further reading.

Part I
What Is Traditional Witchcraft?

Here you stand before a dirt path that stretches and winds far into the distance. On either side of you sit two low stone walls, both time-worn and covered in green moss. All around them grow abundant sprays of foxglove, datura, and belladonna. You notice a forked staff leaning against one of the walls and a large cast-iron cauldron resting on the ground near the other. As the waxing crescent moon breaks through the clouds, you hear the sudden howling of a coyote from somewhere far away. You take in a deep breath, readying yourself for the long journey you are about to begin. You know that it will be challenging and require hard work, but you can already feel your inner power awakening to the beckoning call of what lies ahead. Intuitively grabbing ahold of the staff, you take one last look around before stepping onto the Crooked Path of Traditional Witchcraft.

Chapter 1
DEFINING
TRADITIONAL WITCHCRAFT

What is Traditional Witchcraft? If you're reading this book, it's likely that you are searching for the answer to this very question. Traditional Witchcraft is often described as a *Crooked Path*. The term *crooked* here refers to a number of things. First, it hints at the moral ambiguity classically associated with Witchcraft. Traditional Witches practice magic that is double-edged, capable of both helping and harming. Second, it describes the slightly off-kilter worldview of Traditional Witches, which allows us to see the hidden realm of spirits. Third, it illustrates the Traditional Witches' vacillated movements as we snake between the wild natural landscape and the mysterious Otherworld. Finally, it points to the fact that Traditional Witchcraft is an incredibly difficult practice to succinctly define. There are very few straightforward answers to be given on this path, and those who walk it must be prepared to seek out their own truths. That being said, Traditional Witchcraft can generally be defined as an umbrella term that covers an array of non-Wiccan forms of Witchcraft that are influenced and inspired by folklore.

Over the last several years there has been a steadily growing interest in Traditional Witchcraft, although this is not to say that people have never been interested in it before or that it is somehow a new phenomenon. In fact, the popularity of Traditional Witchcraft has spiked every now and then for the last several decades. It's a path that has always had a beckoning call to people—including those who are new to the Craft and those who are seasoned practitioners—who are seeking more visceral and intuitive forms of Witchcraft. These are people who are being moved to forge a practice that is rooted in folklore as well as one that is focused on the natural world and working intimately with spirits. Today, though, Traditional Witchcraft has reached new levels, and more books and articles on the topic have been written than ever before. You can search the internet and are bound to come across countless websites dedicated to Traditional Witchcraft. Social media has taken it to even greater heights, with Instagram and Tumblr being flooded with pictures and posts regarding #TraditionalWitchcraft.

However, despite the wealth of informative resources being produced, it seems that we are still missing a cohesive definition of what Traditional Witchcraft is and what it entails. Without such a definition, outsiders are frequently left confused and insiders find themselves at a loss for how to concisely describe their own path to others. In hopes to remedy this ambiguity, we must create a new, working definition of Traditional Witchcraft. In order to successfully accomplish this, though, we will need to take a close look at the key beliefs and practices commonly found along the Crooked Path. But first, it will prove most helpful to our cause if we examine some of the reasons it has been so difficult to accurately define Traditional Witchcraft in the first place.

What Makes This Witchcraft "Traditional"?

One of the main challenges we face on our quest to defining Traditional Witchcraft is first being tasked with defining the term *traditional*. What exactly constitutes a tradition or makes something traditional? From my own observations, it would seem that many people tend to define *traditional* as something that is extremely old and that has remained completely unchanged over a long course of time. However, in actuality this definition is incredibly limited and unrealistic, particularly when it comes to Witchcraft.

First and foremost, traditions are not inherently defined by their age. We know that new traditions are being developed all the time. Traditions are simply created when we decide to mindfully and intentionally repeat a certain action, such as going out for coffee with a friend on Sunday mornings or cooking a special dish on a particular holiday. While it's true that long-standing traditions naturally incur a greater sense of salience due to the longer amount of time they've had to impact people's lives, this doesn't negate the significance and value of newer traditions. Secondly, traditions are not static but rather fluid in nature. They are living, breathing things that are added to and subtracted from each time they pass hands, continuously shifting and growing. That's how traditions are kept alive. Change is important because if a tradition becomes stagnant, sooner or later it will become outdated and eventually die off altogether. Moreover, traditions are not created in a vacuum. Instead, they almost always arise from or in response to other already established customs. When it comes to Witchcraft, this means that there is no one "pure" tradition that has developed and remained uninfluenced by other external sources.

Given the common misconceptions about what qualifies as a tradition, Traditional Witchcraft is often mistakenly thought of as representing (or trying to represent) a singular, unified, and unchanged tradition that stretches far back into the mists of time. But this just isn't the case. Instead, the term *Traditional Witchcraft* refers to a collection of different paths that are influenced and inspired by traditions found within folklore. And again, these traditions are subject to change and growth in order for them to have relevance and meaning in the world today. Traditional Witches take stock of the traditions and customs from folklore, particularly that of our ancestors, but we don't fool ourselves into believing that we live in the past or that these traditions have been untouched by the hands of time. Instead, we find ways to weave strands of the past into the tapestry of our modern lives. It is this process that makes Traditional Witchcraft "traditional."

The Use of Folklore in Traditional Witchcraft

While acknowledging the significant role that folklore plays within Traditional Witchcraft, many people still wonder about the validity of its use when establishing a magical practice. Folklore is often associated with fiction and subsequently written off as nothing more than make-believe or fantasy. Consequently, it is natural that questions arise regarding the legitimacy of beliefs and practices that are based on its premise. But consider for a moment that Witchcraft itself is just as often associated with make-believe and fantasy. Like folklore, Witches exist in the liminal space between fact and fiction, and it is part of our unique skill set to take the fantastic and transmute it into reality. Additionally, folklore often contains valuable lessons about a variety of topics—including the practice of Witchcraft—hidden within the folds of its narrative. Therefore, in Traditional Witchcraft, we tap into the stories of folklore as a means of learning more about working magic and connecting with the world of spirits. These lessons are then distilled into an effective, workable practice. And so, while the lore from which our practices are drawn may not represent complete historical truths, it is nonetheless valuable in that it brings meaning and magic to our lives.

Of all the existing folklore, it is that which comes from the surviving records of the European and American Witch Trials that has a particular influence over Traditional Witchcraft. That being said, it's important to note and recognize right away that it remains highly unlikely that those persecuted were practicing Witches. While there are a handful of cases in which it would appear that the accused had some knowledge of working with magic and spirits, we will never know for sure if they were really practitioners of Witchcraft. The confessions given by the accused were frequently obtained under torture, almost certainly driven by a desire to escape pain and death. Therefore, their historical veracity is questionable at best. However, it is not the factual merit of the confessions that interests Traditional Witches but rather the rich body of folklore that they encapsulated and have further generated throughout time.

Regardless of whether or not any of the accused were genuine Witches, it would appear that the elements of Witchcraft contained within their confessions (e.g., use of magical spells, ownership of familiar spirits, meetings of Witches known as *Sabbaths*, and allyship with the Devil) originated from some pre-existing folklore. These elements can be found throughout countless individual confessions all across Europe and America, hinting at an already well-developed set of beliefs regarding Witchcraft and magic. In this way, it seems more than likely that confession materials pertaining to specific Witchcraft practices were not mere fabrications but rather products of a prior established system of folkloric beliefs and ideas. Again, this folklore may not hold weight in terms of historical accuracy, but it has proven to be useful in its ability to inform and inspire the creation of effective modern Witchcraft practices.

Authenticity and the Traditional Witch

Closely intertwined with the preconceived notions about what qualifies something as traditional are ideas regarding what it means for something to be authentic. Authenticity is a highly contentious topic within Traditional Witchcraft as well as the wider Pagan, Witchcraft, and Wiccan community. People have been known to go to great lengths in order to establish a sense of authenticity both within themselves and in their path. Some people will make up wild claims to back up their Craft, like inventing fictional family members to demonstrate a supposed hereditary line of Witches. Others will tear down the practices of fellow Witches in order to feel superior or more powerful. Of course, like the classic school bully, this behavior is usually masking deep insecurities about their own level of knowledge and magical ability. Moreover, their behavior is frequently exacerbated by misguided ideas about what determines authenticity.

Authenticity is often misunderstood as being something that originates from external factors (e.g., money, popularity, personal appearance/aesthetics, etc.). Within the world of Witchcraft and magic, authenticity is most commonly misattributed to age. Similar to the beliefs pertaining to traditions, it is thought that in order for something—in this case a tradition of Witchcraft—to have authenticity, it must be significantly old and have remained unchanged over time. Unfortunately, the sentiment that authenticity comes from age—or any other external factor for that matter—can prove to be quite unhelpful and ultimately lead to disappointment. This is because, in the practice of Traditional Witchcraft, authenticity comes from two places, neither of which are inherently related to age. First, it comes from within, from having a firm belief and confidence in yourself and in your Craft. Second, authenticity comes from effectiveness, or having the ability to successfully work magic and to connect with the spirits. If you feel assured in your magical abilities, if you feel closely knit with the spirits with whom you work, and if your practice brings fulfillment and happiness to your life, then it is an authentic one. In sum, as said by brilliant Witch and author Laura Tempest Zakroff, "The authentic path of Witchcraft is the one that works."[2]

Key Elements of Traditional Witchcraft

Now that we've worked through the initial issues of defining Traditional Witchcraft, it's time to explore the foundations of its practice. Boiled down to the barest of bones, there are three key elements of Traditional Witchcraft, all of which are infused with the folklore we just discussed. At first glance, these elements may

---

2. Laura Tempest Zakroff, *Weave the Liminal: Living Modern Traditional Witchcraft* (Woodbury, MN: Llewellyn Publications, 2019), 48.

seem overly simple, but I encourage you to look deeper (and we will do just that in upcoming chapters). Each element contains many additional threads which, when spun together, create the highly diverse entity that is Traditional Witchcraft. For our purposes of developing a working definition of Traditional Witchcraft, it's pertinent that we now follow these threads back to the very heart that lies at its center.

Working with Magic

Traditional Witchcraft is a path that involves the use of magic through rituals and spells. Like members of traditions such as ceremonial magic, Wicca, and Hoodoo, we tap into various sources of magical power in order to effect change in the world. The way in which magic is employed varies from one practitioner to the next, but many Traditional Witches make use of what is known as *low magic* or *folk magic*—a type of magic that is highly practical and down-to-earth. Just the same, there are also Traditional Witches whose magical practices are more ceremonial in nature, characterized by the use of elaborate rituals featuring a number of special tools and lengthy invocations. While the specifics of how magic is used tend to differ, there are a few key ritual practices that are commonly used, including the compass round (creating a liminal ritual space), treading the mill (creating a trance state and raising magical power), and the housel (giving offerings to spirits). We will discuss these rituals and the art of spellcraft in part 2 of this book.

Working with the Otherworld

The Traditional Witch is one who visits the Otherworld and works with the various types of spirits who reside there. These spirits include gods and ancestors as well as familiar and fetch spirits. While spirits play a prominent role in Traditional Witchcraft, not all practitioners will work with each type of spirit. For example, there are plenty of Traditional Witches who don't acknowledge any sort of deity and instead focus exclusively on their ancestors. For the purpose of simplicity and inclusivity, the generic term *spirits* will be used in this book to encompass all forms, unless otherwise specifically stated. Regardless of the type of spirit, the relationship we have with them is experienced as one of equal partnership and not subjugated worship. We don't bow to our spirits nor do we beg for their help. We actively engage with them, giving offerings, making pacts, and conversing with one another. Establishing working relationships with the spirits is important in Traditional Witchcraft, as they are invaluable guides and magical assistants. In order to develop relationships with spirits, Traditional Witches frequently visit the Otherworld via the practice of hedge-crossing, which is crossing freely back and forth between our world and that of the spirits. We will discuss the Otherworld and how to get there, as well as the various kinds of spirits and how to work with them, in part 3 of this book.

Working with the Natural World

Within the Witchcraft, Wiccan, and Pagan community, nature is viewed as being incredibly sacred and magical. This is particularly true for the Traditional Witch, as our practices are rooted firmly within the natural world, including both our own local landscape and skies above. In Traditional Witchcraft we focus on working with the plants, stones, and animals that are present within our own bioregion, along with the shifting seasonal tides, weather patterns, and planetary influences. We view the world through an animistic lens, meaning that we see the spirit in all these things. The land itself is experienced as a living, breathing entity, often referred to as the genius loci, or spirit of place. Additionally, we work with the individual land wights, or nature spirits, who inhabit the landscape and collectively make up that spirit of place. Just like with the Otherworld and its denizens, when we forge a relationship with the natural world and the spirits who live alongside us, we partner with powerful allies and teachers. We will discuss working with the natural world in part 4 of this book.

All three of these elements are pulled together and infused with folkloric inspiration. This is the Crooked Path of the Traditional Witch, one that wields the forces of magic, ventures into the Otherworldly realm of spirits, and works with the powers of the natural world. The Traditional Witch is one who is informed and inspired by the stories of the past, taken from fact, fiction, and all the places in between. We are spiritual alchemists, collecting and transforming what we find into something that fits our needs and feeds our soul. We will discuss uniting the elements of Traditional Witchcraft in order to build your own personal practice in part 5 of this book.

Religion or Spiritual Practice?

You may have noticed at this point that I have yet to use the term *religion* or *spirituality* in describing Traditional Witchcraft. That's because it is first and foremost a magical practice. Witches work operatively, casting spells and performing rituals in order to effect change in our lives and in the lives of others. It's into our magical practice that we may incorporate religious or spiritual components. This means that at its core, Traditional Witchcraft is non-denominational. Yet, people tend to get into long debates about whether Traditional Witchcraft is a religion or spirituality (or both or neither!). In actuality, there is no right or wrong side to this debate. Instead, it's something that is ultimately up to the individual to determine for themselves and will be based largely on how they conceptualize and differentiate between religion and spirituality.

For many, the word *religion* calls to mind images of grand churches, stuffy sermons, and strict sets of moral rules. Religion is typically thought of as something that is organized or institutionalized, with members following the same system of beliefs and practices that revolve around the worship of a particular deity. Additionally, religion is usually thought to be experienced externally, with divinity being somewhere far away from humankind. If we are to go by this criteria, Traditional Witchcraft doesn't fit all that well into the religious category. In fact, many people protest labeling it as a religion because, as stated earlier, we don't worship our spirits in the sense that a Christian might worship Jesus. Instead, there is a sense of equal footing, with the relationship being a symbiotic partnership in which everyone benefits. Of course, this is beside the fact that not all Traditional Witches work with deities. Furthermore, excluding a few unifying commonalities, there is very little organization within Traditional Witchcraft, with practices varying widely between different cultures, regions, individuals, and specific traditions.

For these reasons, many people feel that Traditional Witchcraft, if anything, is more of a spirituality than a religion. Spirituality is frequently defined as a path that includes working with spirits but in a more autonomous fashion. The relationships with spirits feel more personal, with the individual being able to explore and engage in a way that aligns more with their specific needs and preferences. Moreover, spirituality isn't organized or bound by a universal doctrine, instead leaving it up to the individual to discover what is true for them. In this way, spirituality, as opposed to religion, is experienced on a more internal level. Whether you view Traditional Witchcraft as a religion or spirituality, it's pertinent to keep in mind that what is true for you may not be true for everyone else. Therefore, while you may experience Traditional Witchcraft as a spirituality, someone else may experience it as a religion. We all have diverse beliefs and backgrounds, and respect for these individual differences goes a long way within the world of Witchcraft.

The idea that Traditional Witchcraft is non-denominational, or that it isn't inherently attached to any one religion or spirituality, may be controversial in that we almost always associate Witchcraft exclusively with Paganism. However, Traditional Witchcraft makes use of folk magic, which has historically been dual faith. For example, Traditional Witches often turn to the spells and charms of the Cunning Folk (early magical practitioners in the British Isles), which contain pieces of Christian imagery mixed with bits of Pagan folk belief. A fascinating instance of this blending of faiths is preserved in a folk charm for preventing ague in which three horseshoes are nailed to the foot of one's bed while reciting the following charm:

> *Father, Son, and Holy Ghost,*
> *Nail the devil to this post.*
> *Thrice I strike with holy crook,*
> *One for God and one for Wod and one for Lok.*[3]

In this case, the Witch is actively calling upon both Christian figures and the Norse deities Woden and Loki. Today, you will find Traditional Witches who continue the practice of dual-faith observance. For example, many practitioners will not hesitate to call upon Catholic saints and use psalms in their spellwork. If you wish to flavor your personal path with parts of a specific religion or spirituality, that is your choice to make.

A Working Definition

Thus far we've established what it means to be traditional and authentic, why folklore is a valid and important source of information, what the key elements

---

3. Christina Hole, *Witchcraft in England* (London: B. T. Batsford, 1947), 134.

of Traditional Witchcraft practice are, and that it can be either a religion or spirituality. At this point, it's time to use what we've learned to create our working definition of Traditional Witchcraft:

> *Traditional Witchcraft is an umbrella term that covers a vast array of non-Wiccan practices that are inspired by folklore. These practices may be viewed as religious or spiritual depending upon the group or individual practitioner. Traditional Witches focus on the use of magic, connecting with the natural landscape, and working with various spirits in both the physical realm and the Otherworld.*

 ### EXERCISE 1:
Personally Defining Traditional Witchcraft

Purpose: To consider how, given what you've learned thus far, you personally define Traditional Witchcraft.

Location: A quiet space where you can think and write.

Time: Anytime.

Tools: Your journal and a pen.

In your journal, respond to the following question:

+ Do you agree with the definition of Traditional Witchcraft provided at the end of this chapter? If yes, in what ways does it resonate with your own experiences, feelings, or ideas? If no, how would you personally define Traditional Witchcraft?

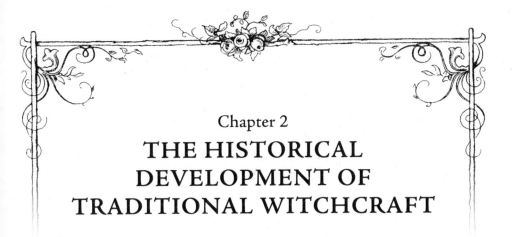

Chapter 2
THE HISTORICAL DEVELOPMENT OF TRADITIONAL WITCHCRAFT

The world of Witchcraft would be forever changed by two events that took place in England during 1951. First, the Witchcraft Act of 1735 was repealed, effectively decriminalizing Witchcraft. This act had replaced the previous laws, under which Witchcraft was classified as a capital offense, punishable by death. With the Age of Enlightenment, belief in the reality of Witchcraft had faded considerably. Instead, it was thought that those who claimed to have magical powers were merely scam artists looking to con people out of their money and material goods. Thus, under the 1735 law, it was illegal to claim to have magical powers. Anyone caught doing so was susceptible to being punished with heavy fines or imprisonment. But in 1951 this changed when it was replaced with the Fraudulent Mediums Act, which specifically targeted those falsely claiming to be psychic in order to make money (the Fraudulent Mediums Act was in turn repealed in May 2008). With Witchcraft no longer illegal, people could be more open about it—both in practice and in writing—without fear of legal consequences. Although, it would still be many years before Witchcraft gained any semblance of societal acceptance.

Cecil Williamson and Gerald Gardner
The legalization of Witchcraft opened the way for the second major event, which was the opening of the Folklore Centre of Superstition and Witchcraft in Castletown on the Isle of Man. The Centre, which was housed in an old windmill, was

owned and run by a man named Cecil Williamson. Truly an unsung hero in the history of modern Witchcraft, Williamson never wrote any books or sought media attention (at least not to the extreme that many of his contemporaries did). Instead he spent his time collecting the stories and artifacts of those he lovingly referred to as "Aunty Mays" or "Wayside Witches." It is through his curation of a vast collection of magical documents and artifacts that so many of their stories have been kept alive. Williamson himself was quite vague about his own personal involvement with Witchcraft, typically giving ambiguous responses when questioned. Though, sometime after his death, a manuscript written in his hand, simply titled *Witchcraft*, was discovered. In it were various spells and rituals that were dictated in such a way that suggested he had made use of them himself.[4]

Shortly after the opening of the Folklore Centre of Superstition and Witchcraft, *The Sunday Pictorial* ran an article that discussed the Centre's resident Witch, Gerald Gardner. This was quite significant, as Gardner was one of the first people to publicly come forward as a practitioner of Witchcraft since its decriminalization in Britain. According to his claims, Gardner had been initiated into an pre-existing coven of Witches in the New Forest area of England during 1939.[5] Utilizing the fragmentary information he received from the coven, along with elements of folk and ceremonial magic, he effectively formed his own tradition of Witchcraft (what would later become known as Wicca). Williamson and Gardner met briefly in 1947 at the Atlantis bookshop in London and formed a tentative acquaintanceship. Later on, Gardner showed up at the Centre (accounts of his arrival are widely varied) and became business partners with Williamson. Unfortunately, the relationship between the two was tumultuous and short-lived, characterized by frequent fighting regarding finances. In fact, Williamson believed that Gardner was actively attempting to take over the business.[6]

Eventually, the two men experienced a complete falling out and Williamson ended up selling the Centre to Gardner before returning to the mainland. Undeterred, Williamson set about trying to open a new museum, creating several incarnations before finally settling in Boscastle, England. There he established the

4. Steve Patterson, *Cecil Williamson's Book of Witchcraft* (London: Troy Books, 2014).
5. Ronald Hutton, *Triumph of the Moon* (New York: Oxford University Press, 1999), 205–6.
6. Michael Howard, *Modern Wicca* (Woodbury, MN: Llewellyn Publications, 2010), 103.

Museum of Witchcraft and Magic where it still stands today. Meanwhile, Gardner continued over the next several years to bring his brand of Witchcraft into the mainstream. During this time, though, there were other Witches who were growing displeased with what he was presenting to the public as Witchcraft. In their opinion, Gardner's vision of the Craft did not align with their own beliefs and practices. The rising tension continued to boil under the surface until Gardner's death in February of 1964.

Robert Cochrane and the Clan of Tubal Cain

In October of that same year, the Witchcraft Research Association (WRA) was launched in England with the goal of uniting the members of various Craft traditions. Ironically though, it ended up being a platform for divisive conflict, particularly through its newsletter, *Pentagram*. The second issue of the newsletter featured an article titled "Witchcraft Today," in which the author, Robert Cochrane (whose real name was actually Roy Bowers), falsely claimed to belong to a family of hereditary Witches and vehemently rejected Gardner's ideas about Witchcraft.[7] In fact, it was Cochrane himself who coined the term *Gardnerian*, which was originally meant as an insult to those who followed Gardner's tradition. Interestingly enough, despite his obsessional dislike for Gardner, there is evidence to suggest that Cochrane had at some point received a first-degree initiation into Gardnerian Wicca.[8]

Cochrane created his own tradition of Witchcraft in the early 1960s, which became known as the Clan of Tubal Cain—named after the biblical blacksmith. Because Cochrane never authored any books, most of what we know about the beliefs and practices of his tradition comes from the few articles he published. Additionally, after Cochrane's tragic suicide in 1966, a number of letters he had written to other magical practitioners became available to the public, which shed further light upon his tradition. Cochrane believed that Witchcraft was one of the last remaining mystery traditions in the world, with Witches being mystics in search of the ultimate wisdom—the understanding of the gods and one's own inherent

---

7. Robert Cochrane, "Witchcraft Today," in *The Roebuck in the Thicket: An Anthology of the Robert Cochrane Witchcraft Tradition*, ed. Michael Howard (Somerset, UK: Capall Bann Publishing, 2001), 56–59.

8. Michael Howard, *Children of Cain* (Richmond Vista, CA: Three Hands Press, 2011), 60.

divinity. He was also a firm advocate for the fluidity of Witchcraft practices and the need to contextualize them in a way that fits with modernity.[9] Within his tradition, veneration was given to both a god (known by various names, including Tubal Cain) and a goddess (known primarily as Fate or the Pale-Faced Goddess), as well as their cosmic offspring, known as the Horn Child. Cochrane's coven was led by a Magister and a Maiden (or Magistra). The coven typically met out of doors in some desolate and wild area, and the rituals performed were usually ecstatic and unscripted in nature. It is from Cochrane's tradition that we receive the three common rituals used in Traditional Witchcraft—the compass round, treading the mill, and the housel.

Although Cochrane's character and his claims were dubious at times, many people were greatly affected by his work. As noted by Professor Ronald Hutton, "If he actually did compose all the rituals and their underpinning ideas himself, then the word for him is surely not 'charlatan,' but 'genius.'"[10] Whether he was a fraud or not, it is clear that Cochrane's style of Witchcraft worked well, and it would go on to influence a number of emerging traditions, including the continuation of the Clan of Tubal Cain. These traditions have further propagated the concepts and practices that he popularized. It is truly a mystery what Traditional Witchcraft would look like today without the work of Robert Cochrane.

Doreen Valiente

In September of 1952, Cecil Williamson was featured in an article entitled "Witchcraft in Britain," which was published in the magazine *Illustrated*. Having read the article, a woman named Doreen Valiente wrote to Williamson inquiring about the article's mention of a coven of Witches operating in Southern Britain. Williamson responded by forwarding the letter along to Gerald Gardner, who subsequently met with Valiente. At Midsummer of 1953, she was initiated into Gardner's coven.[11] During the following years, Valiente rose to become the coven's High Priestess. However, she became increasingly vexed with Gardner's attempts to gain publicity, which she viewed as a harmful violation of the coven's

---

9. Cochrane, "Witchcraft Today," in *The Roebuck in the Thicket*, 56–59.

10. Hutton, *Triumph of the Moon*, 316.

11. Philip Heselton, *Doreen Valiente Witch* (Woodbury, MN: Llewellyn Publications, 2016), 67–73.

privacy. In attempts to salvage the coven, which was splitting into two factions (those who supported Gardner's desire for publicity and those who did not), Valiente penned a list of proposed coven rules that were intended to protect the integrity and anonymity of the coven and its members. However, Gardner rejected these rules and produced his own, which, to Valiente's great displeasure, set out to limit the power of the High Priestess.[12] Infuriated, Valiente broke away from Gardner's coven in 1957.

After the split, Valiente continued to explore different forms of Witchcraft, and in 1964 she met Robert Cochrane. According to her own account, she was quite impressed with his charisma as well as his preference for outdoor rituals and staying out of the public eye. And so, on Halloween night of 1964, she was initiated into Cochrane's coven. However, despite her satisfaction with Cochrane's vision of Witchcraft, she quickly became displeased with his personal character. Valiente was skeptical about his claims to belong to a family lineage of Witches and was growing increasingly annoyed with his unrelenting disdain for Gardner. This came to a head when Cochrane jokingly called for a "Night of the Long Knives" (referring to a series of political executions ordered by Adolf Hitler in 1934) with the Gardnerians. Fed up with his grudge against Gardner and disgusted by the suggestion of violence, Valiente told Cochrane off and left his coven shortly thereafter.[13]

Doreen Valiente is an immensely important figure in the history of modern Witchcraft for many reasons, among them being her writing on the subjects of both Wicca and Traditional Witchcraft. Some of Valiente's most impressive and long-lasting contributions to Gardner's coven, and the future Wiccan community, were her poetic revisions to the existing ritual liturgy, including those she made to the invocation known as "The Charge of the Goddess." Moreover, Valiente helped bring information regarding Traditional Witchcraft to the wider public through her book *The Rebirth of Witchcraft*, which included three chapters devoted to the topic. She went on to co-author a book with Evan John Jones (who had also been a member of Cochrane's Clan of Tubal Cain) titled *Witchcraft: A Tradition Renewed*. In this book, Jones provided his unique version of Traditional Witchcraft,

---

12. Hutton, *Triumph of the Moon*, 249.

13. Doreen Valiente, *The Rebirth of Witchcraft* (London: Robert Hale, 1989), 129.

which is noticeably influenced by the work of both Cochrane and Gardner. Just as she had done before in Gardner's coven, Valiente put her poetry skills to use in providing the invocations to go along with Jones's rituals. Both books contain invaluable information regarding the early development and practice of Traditional Witchcraft as well as further demonstrating the considerable and far-reaching role that Doreen Valiente has played in the world of Witchcraft.

1734, Feri, and American Traditional Witchcraft

Featured in the final issue of the *Pentagram* newsletter was a personal advertisement written by an American man named Joseph B. Wilson who was seeking contact with anyone interested in the "Old Religion." Incidentally, it was Robert Cochrane who replied to Wilson's advertisement, hoping to establish contact with Traditional Witches who may have emigrated from Britain to the United States.[14] Throughout the six letters he penned, Cochrane used cryptic references and riddles to teach Wilson more about his tradition of Witchcraft. In his third letter, Cochrane elaborated, "We teach by poetic inference, by thinking along lines that belong to the world of dreams and images."[15] One of the first questions he asked of Wilson was whether or not he understood the order of 1734, which he later explained was not a specific date but rather a coded message that held meaning to certain Witches.[16] Eventually, it was determined that 1734 was actually the numerical representation of the Black Goddess, or Fate herself. Using the tree alphabet found within Robert Graves's book *The White Goddess* (which had a huge influence on Cochrane's Craft), Wilson discovered that 1734 translated to the name Hio (pronounced I-OH).[17] 1734 would later become the namesake of Wilson's own tradition.

Prior to the advertisement, Wilson had already been exploring Witchcraft and magic, guided by a friend whom he referred to as "Sean." Under Sean's men-

---

14. Howard, *Children of Cain*, 64.

15. Robert Cochrane, "Letter Three," in *The Robert Cochrane Letters: An Insight into Modern Traditional Witchcraft*, ed. Michael Howard (Somerset, UK: Capall Bann Publishing, 2002), 26.

16. Robert Cochrane, "Letter Two," in *The Robert Cochrane Letters: An Insight into Modern Traditional Witchcraft*, ed. Michael Howard (Somerset, UK: Capall Bann Publishing, 2002), 23.

17. Joseph B. Wilson, "Those Pesky Riddles," 1734 Witchcraft, accessed April 30, 2019, http://www.1734-witchcraft.org/riddles.html.

torship, Wilson was taught a mixture of folk magic, psychic development, and Native American spirituality. Wilson was able to use this knowledge to help augment the information he had been given by Cochrane. Regrettably, due to Cochrane's untimely death, Wilson was never able to meet him in person. However, in 1969 he was sent overseas as part of the United States Air Force, during which time he met with several people who had known and worked with Cochrane. One of the most influential of these people was Ruth Wynn-Owen, who shared with Wilson information regarding her tradition Y Plant Bran (the Family of Bran). Upon returning to the United States, Wilson bound together the information he had learned from Cochrane, Sean, and Wynn-Owen and created the 1734 tradition.[18] Wilson's work inspired the development of further American permutations of Traditional Witchcraft, including a group known as the Roebuck Tradition, which was established by a couple named Ann and Dave Finnin.

Another strand of American Traditional Witchcraft is known today as the Feri tradition. Feri was developed during the 1960s by a couple named Victor and Cora Anderson. According to his account, Victor was initiated into Witchcraft when he was nine years old by a woman who claimed to be a faerie. Later, in 1932, Victor was initiated into a group of Witches known as the Harpy coven. Victor described the coven's focus as a mixture of folk magic and Huna (a set of spiritual practices and beliefs inspired by Hawaiian tradition). Twelve years later, Victor met Cora and the two started their own group, which was notably inspired by Huna, Vodoun, Kabbalah, Native American spirituality, Appalachian folk magic, and the Yazidi people. The Andersons' coven would grow into what is now the Feri tradition of Witchcraft. Although, it should be noted that Victor never saw himself as the founder of Feri, instead envisioning himself as a grandmaster of a pre-existing tradition.[19]

Feri is an initiatory tradition and is often described as ecstatic in nature, with rituals focused on embracing sexuality and expressions of self. Veneration is given to two primary deities (although there are several more who exist within this tradition), known as the Star Goddess and her cosmic child, the Blue God, who

---

18. Howard, *Children of Cain*, 64–67.

19. Storm Faerywolf, *Betwixt & Between* (Woodbury, MN: Llewellyn Publications, 2017), 19–23.

is alternately called both Dian Y Glas and Melek Ta'us.[20] An important component of the Feri tradition is the belief that we are each composed of three-souls—referred to as the fetch, talker, and holy daemon—with whom balanced communication is necessary in order to work magic and reach our full human and spiritual potential.[21] Feri remains a flourishing tradition to this day, with many different lineages existing across the world.

Traditional Witchcraft versus Wicca

Due to their historical relationship, it's inevitable that when discussing Traditional Witchcraft, we must tackle the question of how it relates to Wicca. It's a fair question given that for the longest time, Wicca has predominantly been the front and center of the modern Witchcraft movement. The question of how these two paths differ from each other is one that is highly debated. Presently, and in the past, this debate has been ensconced in contention that typically arises in response to claims that one path is more authentic than the other. On one side you have Traditional Witches condemning Wicca as "watered-down Witchcraft" or "Witchcraft without teeth." On the other you have Wiccans who denounce Traditional Witchcraft as being made-up or a cheap imitation of Wicca itself. In reality, though, both the criticisms regarding Wicca and Traditional Witchcraft are almost entirely founded on stereotypes and misinformation.

For example, some people view Wicca as a weak form of Witchcraft because it is commonly purported that Wiccans are prohibited from working acts of baneful or harmful magic such as hexing or cursing. The Wiccan Rede ("An it harm none, do what ye will") and Threefold Law (whatever energy you put out, good or bad, returns to you threefold) are frequently cited as evidence to back this belief, as they are thought to expressly forbid baneful workings. However, as Gardnerian High Priestess Thorn Mooney points out, "Though the Wiccan Rede and Threefold Law have so long been promoted as universalities—essential beliefs that define all Wiccan practitioners—this has never *actually* been the case."[22] Thus, many Wiccans do, in fact, make use of hexing and cursing when the need

---

20. Howard, *Children of Cain*, 179.

21. Storm Faerywolf, *Betwixt & Between* (Woodbury, MN: Llewellyn Publications, 2017), 51–53.

22. Thorn Mooney, *Traditional Wicca: A Seeker's Guide* (Woodbury, MN: Llewellyn Publications, 2018), 96.

arises. On the flip side, the view of Traditional Witchcraft as a fabricated path is typically based on misunderstandings about the nature of traditions and the usefulness of folklore as discussed earlier.

The assertion that Traditional Witchcraft is just another version of Wicca, but perhaps with a spooky veneer, is primarily false. However, there are noticeable overlaps and similarities between the two that are worth discussing. In the historical development of both paths, there are certainly areas in which they have had influence over one another. For instance, Gardner would have been undoubtedly inspired by the Witchcraft and folk magic practices preserved in Williamson's museum. Moreover, in augmenting his growing tradition, Gardner pulled from folk and ceremonial magic—both sources that bolster the practices of Traditional Witches. Cochrane received a first-degree initiation into Wicca, and Valiente would have naturally brought further Wiccan ideas with her when she joined the Clan of Tubal Cain. The blending of these paths still occurs today, with Wiccans incorporating parts of Traditional Witchcraft into their practices and vice versa. It's natural that these two paths would influence one another and even blend in certain areas because, when it comes down to it, they are both forms of Witchcraft. Like two tree trunks growing from the same base (Witchcraft), Traditional Witchcraft and Wicca share the same roots (e.g., folk and ceremonial magic). However, despite their shared foundation, the two paths branch out in different directions.

Given the contention and the fact that both Traditional Witchcraft and Wicca are ultimately two sides of the same coin, many find attempts to differentiate the two useless and divisive. So why bother at all? Well, it so happens that our minds are naturally programmed to sort information into categories, to make note of differences and similarities in order to create meaning and understanding about the world around us. We understand that dogs and cats are both mammals, but they are different species. We understand that Traditional Witchcraft and Wicca are both types of Witchcraft, but they are different paths. Additionally, focusing on differences isn't intrinsically negative—it just depends on how we choose to respond to those differences. Do we celebrate them or do we use them as weapons against one another? As history shows, the differences between Traditional Witchcraft and Wicca have been used to fuel battles over a false sense of authenticity and power. However, it doesn't need to be this way moving forward. Differences make us unique but don't make us inherently better than anyone else. Identifying the differences—and similarities, for that matter—between Traditional Witchcraft and Wiccan needn't be an antagonistic act, so long as we can check our egos and have mutual respect for one another.

That being said, some of the main differences between Traditional Witchcraft and Wicca include specific rituals performed, magical tools used, coven structure, and solitary work. Wicca, at least in its traditional initiatory form (Gardnerian and Alexandrian), involves specific rituals (e.g., casting a circle, raising a cone of power, and the sharing of cakes and ale) that are unique to its practice. These rites, although varying slightly from coven to coven, normally follow a set of standard gestures and words that remain mostly consistent over time. As will be demonstrated in part 2 of this book, the rituals and spells in Traditional Witchcraft tend to be more ecstatic in nature, with gestures and words coming spontaneously from the heart. There are also rituals that are particular to Traditional Witchcraft, including the compass round, treading the mill, and the housel. The tools used in Traditional Witchcraft rituals also differ, with the stang (a forked ritual staff) being the most popular, as opposed to the athame (a double-edged ritual knife) used in Wicca. Moreover, while there are Traditional Witches who work within coven systems, many prefer to work alone. Meanwhile, Wicca is a coven-based path in which you must be initiated in order to become a member. When Traditional Witches do work in covens, they typically don't involve a degree system or utilize the same titles and roles, such as High Priest and High Priestess. Instead, covens are customarily led by a Magister or a Maiden (or Magistra).

In addition to physical ones, there are also differences in some of the core beliefs of Traditional Witchcraft and Wicca. For example, within Wicca there is actually very little emphasis on connecting with the landscape. Nature is experienced symbolically, as a metaphor for the tradition's specific mythos. The Wheel of Year is followed more as a narrative of the gods than as a way to work with and honor the natural world. As already pointed out, Traditional Witchcraft holds a very animistic worldview that stresses the importance of the genius loci and land wights. Our practice is based on bioregionalism, meaning it's centered upon the land we live upon versus that of faraway places. Everything from the plants and stones to the animals and weather patterns is considered significant.

Furthermore, in Wicca, communing with the divine usually happens on the physical plane, within the magic circle. The High Priest or High Priestess calls upon the gods, channeling them and bringing them into the circle. For Traditional Witches, we also connect to our spirits on the physical plane but we also visit with them in the Otherworld.

These are only some of the differences between Traditional Witchcraft and Wicca. It's probable that you could come up with many more if you really wanted to, but keep in mind that both paths are highly expansive and encompass many different people and groups. It's nearly impossible to make definite statements about what *all* Traditional Witches or Wiccans do or don't do. Thus, drawing hard lines between them isn't as easy as some would like it to be. And, when it comes down to it, much of what makes Traditional Witchcraft different from Wicca is something that needs to be experienced firsthand. To some, this might sound vague or uninspired, but it's true nonetheless. When I first started studying Traditional Witchcraft, I was skeptical about how it differed from Wicca. However, when I actually began to implement my developing beliefs and practices, I felt the indescribable differences that are there just under the surface.

 EXERCISE 2:
Comparing Traditional Witchcraft and Wicca

Purpose: To reflect upon the similarities and differences between Traditional Witchcraft and Wicca.

Location: A quiet space where you can think and write.

Time: Anytime.

Tools: Your journal and a pen.

In your journal, respond to the following questions:

+ What do you see as the primary differences between Traditional Witchcraft and Wicca?

+ What about the similarities between the two paths?

+ What are some of the stereotypes you may have heard about Traditional Witchcraft and Wicca? Do you think that there is truth in them or do you suspect that they are based on misinformation?

Part II
Working with Magic

Farther down the path, you stumble upon an altar set up on a large old tree stump. You survey the items displayed, which include a knife, a cup, and a plate, with a rustic broomstick standing nearby. Silently, you wonder how each of these tools are to be used. Just ahead, you spot thin wisps of gray smoke emanating from the remains of a bonfire. You notice that the ashes rest in the very center of three concentric rings carved into the ground, perhaps the remnants of some ritual. Closing your eyes, you can imagine a lone Witch dancing around the fire, casting spells and chanting to the moon. The magic in the night air is palpable and you decide to stay for a bit, ready to learn more about the tools, spells, and rituals of Traditional Witchcraft.

Chapter 3
MAGICAL BASICS

Whether it's casting a spell or performing a ritual, working with magic is a fundamental feature of Traditional Witchcraft. Traditional Witches wield the power of magic and use it to achieve our various goals and manifest our deepest desires. Every Witch possesses a cosmic flame within their soul, a burning reservoir of sorcerous power that awaits our call to action. As Witches, by nature, we are also acutely aware of the magical power that exists within the natural world and that can be found in the world beyond. Through a combination of learned skill and innate magical ability, we are able to conjure forth these natural and Otherworldly forces in order to bend and shape the world around us. To learn how to work successful spells and rituals, you must examine the individual components and steps of the magical process—learning to access your own personal power and that of the world around you. But first, in order to use magic with responsibility and respect, it will serve you well to consider magical ethics.

Magical Ethics in Traditional Witchcraft

Within the practice of Traditional Witchcraft, there is no universal set of ethics that determines the appropriate use of magic. There are no inherent binding laws or mandates that forbid certain types of spells and rituals, nor are there restrictions or regulations that dictate if and when magic is to be used at all. However, Traditional Witchcraft should not be mistaken for some sort of magical free-for-all. While we aren't governed by a set of unified ethics, Traditional Witches are subject to personal sovereignty, or self-rule. Each practitioner is ultimately responsible for determining, for themselves, what is right or wrong.

Additionally, the personal ethics of Traditional Witches tend to be flexible and open to situational interpretation. There are very few moral absolutes in Traditional Witchcraft, with certain acts of magic *always* being right and others *always* being wrong. Instead, morality is viewed on a spectrum with most situations falling into the vast space between absolute right and wrong. Therefore, what is magically ethical must be figured out on a case-by-case basis. For example, you might view casting a healing spell on someone without their permission or knowledge as a violation of their consent. Yet, you might find violation of consent morally justifiable in a situation where you need to bind a dangerous enemy. In this example, we can see that what is ethical in one situation may actually be more harmful in another.

Finally, it must be understood that every act of magic has its consequences, both positive and negative. These consequences affect not only the world around us and those within it, but ourselves as well. Regardless of personal beliefs concerning concepts such as karma, it's a magical fact that we are more likely to attract that which we project. If we are working magic that is positive or beneficent, we are going to experience that same energy to some degree on a physical, mental, emotional, and spiritual level. Similarly, when we work magic that is negative or harmful, we are susceptible to feeling that energy as well. Whether our rituals and spells are geared toward blessing or blasting, it behooves us to thoroughly consider the possible negative consequences of our magical workings. As you will see later in this chapter, sometimes even the most positive of intentions can have detrimental repercussions. As a part of being personally sovereign, the Traditional Witch must be prepared to accept full responsibility for their actions and the resulting consequences of their magic.

Baneful Magic

Witches have long been associated with acts of baneful magic, a type of magic that is destructive, restrictive, or otherwise oppositional in nature. Within folklore you will find a plethora of examples of Witches blighting crops, sinking ships, raising storms, inflicting illness, or otherwise magically harming their enemies. This is because, for the longest time (and still today), Witchcraft has been a path largely for the disenfranchised or those who have been marginalized and oppressed. It is a path that offers a way in which individuals can become empowered and take control of our lives. In the case of baneful magic, such acts often provide a way for Witches to take back their power, protect themselves and others, and exact justice or vengeance when necessary.

Baneful magic comes in many flavors and intensities, but most acts can be placed into one of the four following categories:

Curse: An act of magic that causes long-term or permanent harm.

Hex: An act of magic that causes short-term or temporary harm.

Banishing: Magically expelling or doing away with something or someone.

Binding: Magically restraining or incapacitating something or someone.

While it's rare that anyone would go out of their way to cause harm, there are certain situations in which it's necessary. There are times in which we must turn to baneful magic in order to protect ourselves and others, as well as to rise above dangerous or oppressive circumstances. While it's up to the individual practitioner to decide which circumstances constitute the use of baneful magic, remember that magic has consequences. It might not be the case that if you hex someone, you're going to be hexed in return. But consider that when you work baneful magic, you are tapping into darker forces, and those forces might just tap you back. Magic should be approached with respect and responsibility in general, but this is even more important when it comes to the baneful type. Understandably, every situation is different, and you've got to do what you've got to do, but baneful magic is typically best reserved for emergencies or as a last resort. Regardless, the general rule should always be to carefully consider your options, their potential consequences (both to your target and to yourself), and whether or not you're willing to pay the price.

 EXERCISE 3:
Ethics Reflection

Purpose: To reflect upon your own personal magical ethics.

Location: A quiet space where you can think and write.

Time: Anytime.

Tools: Your journal and a pen.

In your journal, respond to the following questions:

+ Do you believe there are situations where malefic magic is justified?
+ Are there any positive aspects to hexing?
+ What do you think are some possible repercussions of hexing?
+ When it comes to hexing, are there certain lines you will not cross?

The Magical Process

Now that we have discussed the ethics of magical practice, it's time to explore how to go about working with the forces of magic. There are two essential components to effectively working magic: your intention and the power necessary to back it up. Your intention is your magical goal or, in other words, what you'd like to make happen. Intention, along with the entire process of working magic, is strengthened with the skill of visualization. The component of power is the magic itself, which is either raised from within or channeled from an outside source. Your combined intent and power are then projected forth to their necessary destination. Altogether, there are four steps to working magic:

1. Determining your magical intention.
2. Visualizing your magical intention.
3. Raising or channeling the necessary magical power.
4. Projecting your combined intent and power.

Intention

Intention is often said to be the cornerstone of any magical working. In order for a spell or ritual to be most successful, there needs to be a clearly defined goal in mind. Having a vague intention will result in a vague outcome, meaning that if your intention is unclear, your magical working will likely be done in vain. In order to avoid magical misfires, you must be specific about what you want, when you want it, and the manner in which you'd like to obtain it. First, you need to elaborate on what it is you desire. Simply saying that you want a "better-paying job" is not enough. A job doing what? A job that pays what amount of money? A job in what geographical location? All these details are necessary; otherwise, you may end up with a better-paying job but one that is in an undesirable career field in an inconvenient location and that only pays slightly more than your current one. Instead you might say, "I want a job within the (specific career) field that pays no less than (specific amount of money) and is no more than (specific distance) away from my home."

Second, you need to include a timeframe in which you'd like your magical intention to manifest. If you don't give a specific time by which you'd like to see results, your intention could come to fruition at any point between tomorrow and the foreseeable future. Instead you might include something like, "My magical intention will come to manifestation by (specific date)."

Third, it's imperative that you include an explanation of how you'd like to attain your desired results. Explicitly outlining how your intention will come to manifest helps prevent unwanted magical consequences. For example, if you were to cast a spell to lose ten pounds but left out the "how," you could end up getting very sick and thus shedding the weight. Instead you might include something along the lines of, "I will lose ten pounds during the next four months by sticking to my healthy diet and exercise plan."

All that being said, while your magical intentions need to be specific, they also need to be realistic and flexible. If you are unrealistic, rigid, or even too specific with your intentions, you will inadvertently limit the probability of success. It's helpful to think of your magical intention like a fishing net. If you cast too wide of a net, you are likely going to catch too many fish or fish that you didn't really want. On the flip side, if you cast too narrow of a net, you are less likely to catch any fish at all.

Visualization

Once you know your magical intention, it's time to take it a step further with visualization. The process of visualization occurs when a specific thought or idea is turned into a clear mental image. For example, you may think of an apple and then proceed to see the fruit within your mind's eye. In addition to seeing an image, you may also touch, hear, smell, and taste it. As such, you may also feel the visualized apple as you hold it, hear yourself bite into its surface, smell its aroma, and taste its flavor. Hence, visualization is a way of not only seeing but also having a full tactile experience with something mentally. This is important when casting spells and performing rituals because when you are able to visualize your intention, you are effectively showing the magic where to go and what to do. In essence, by visualizing your intended outcome, you are creating a target to which magical power can then be sent in order to manifest your desires.

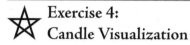

Exercise 4:
Candle Visualization

Purpose: To practice basic visualization by holding the image of a burning candle within your mind's eye.

Location: A quiet, comfortable space.

Time: Anytime.

Tools: None.

To begin, close your eyes and take in a nice deep breath. Exhale, allowing your body and mind to still. When you feel ready, focus your attention on the blank space above and between your two eyes (you can do this by gazing upward with your closed eyes). Call to mind the image of a burning pillar candle and project it onto the blank space. Once the candle is in place, take a closer look at and notice its finer details.

What does the candle look like? What color is it? Is the candle's surface smooth or covered in wax drips? How high does the candle's flame burn? Is the flame flickering or does it stand still? Can you feel the heat of the flame? What does the candle smell like? Does the candle make any noise as it burns?

Try to hold this image for two to three minutes. The more you immerse yourself in the finer details of the visualization, the more effective and powerful it will be.

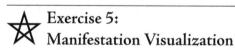

Exercise 5:
Manifestation Visualization

Purpose: To practice visualizing the manifestation of a specific magical intention.

Location: A quiet, comfortable space.

Time: Anytime.

Tools: None.

Before you start this exercise, decide on what it is that you'd like to manifest. When you're ready to begin, close your eyes and take in a nice deep breath. Exhale, allowing your body and mind to still. As in the previous exercise, focus your attention on the blank space above and between your two eyes.

In your mind's eye, picture yourself in a future reality in which your magical intention has already materialized. What does this reality look like? What's happening? For instance, if your goal is to banish an unwanted person, see that person disappearing from your life. Visualize yourself being free from their presence, however it might have been experienced in the past. Next, picture what you'd be doing in this situation. Envision yourself being able to go about your daily life without being troubled by the bothersome individual. Finally, picture how your life (or the lives of others) has been affected by the results of your magic. How do you feel in this situation? Visualize what it would feel like to be free of that person.

Try to remain in this reality for 2 to 3 minutes, increasing your focus on the specific details as you go along. Again, the more you are able to immerse yourself in these details, the more effective and powerful your visualization will be.

Power

Having a clearly defined intention is important when working a spell or ritual, but it's nothing without the magical power necessary to back it up. Power is what fuels our magical workings and turns intentions into results. Where does the power come from? Magic emanates from many places, but broadly speaking, we can access its power from either internal or external sources. Internal power comes from within us. It is the magic that is naturally inherent within each and every Witch. External power, on the other hand, is channeled from sources outside of us. This power can be channeled from natural sources such as plants, stones, planets, weather, and so on. In the case of natural sources, the specific power being accessed is often referred to as *virtue*. External power can also originate from Otherworldly spirits (e.g., gods, ancestors, familiar spirits, etc.).

How do we access power when working magic? In the case of accessing personal power, the magical energy is already alive within you. Your personal power is always at work, but during spells and rituals its intensity must be amplified. There are a number of ways to raise personal power, including visualization and body movement. We can also use our abilities of visualization to tap into our inner power and increase its intensity by envisioning what that power looks and feels like as it grows in strength. Movement of the body—whether it's a simple hand gesture or a frenzied dance—produces energy. When this energy is focused and projected intentionally, it becomes magic. An easy approach to doing this is to rub your hands together vigorously, creating friction, then pulling them apart and feeling the resulting power radiating from your palms. A more complex method of raising personal power through body movement, which will be discussed further in the following chapter, is through the ritual known as treading the mill.

External power can be accessed through two main methods. First, we can channel power present in the natural world. The process of channeling power from nature starts by tuning in to an external source whose magical virtue corresponds with your specific intention. For example, I might channel the virtues of Jupiter to bring me luck, or I might channel the virtues of lavender to promote a sense of calm in my household. The power from these sources is then merged with your own before being directed toward your desired outcome. Second, we can access external power by petitioning spirits for their magical assistance. Petitioning involves approaching a spirit, such as a god, ancestor, or familiar, and asking them for magical help, usually in return for a specific offering (e.g., bread, wine, milk, honey, etc.). The spirit may then proceed to aid your magical working by adding their power to it or by fulfilling your intentions altogether. For instance, your ancestors may lend their power to a ritual for protection, or they may provide you with the protection itself by watching out for your safety. Working magic with Otherworldly spirits will be covered in part 3 of this book.

 EXERCISE 6:
Raising Internal Power

Purpose: To practice raising your own personal magic power.

Location: A quiet, comfortable space.

Time: Anytime.

Tools: None.

To begin, close your eyes and take in a nice deep breath. Exhale, allowing your body and mind to still. Next, visualize that a glowing light swirls within the core of your stomach—this is your inner magical power. The particular color will depend on your personal preference or your specific magical intention (e.g., red for protection, green for luck, blue for healing, etc.).

Once you can see your magical power, visualize that with every inhale, it begins to glow brighter. Breathe in deeply and then exhale. Imagine that the light starts to swirl and spin faster, forming a cyclone of magical energy. Feel the magic building in intensity, like a pulsing electricity. Next, with each exhale, imagine the light is expanding out from your core. Feel the power moving up your chest, spreading down your arms and into your fingertips. Send the magic down your legs and into your toes. Notice how your body vibrates with energy; hold this sensation for a minute or two.

Now, continuing to breathe steadily, slowly pull your magic back. Imagine the light receding from your toes and up your legs, up from your fingertips and arms, coming back to your core. With each breath, feel the energy starting to still, spinning more and more slowly until you have returned to your normal state. If need be, you can also ground yourself by sending any excess energy into the earth where it will be recycled within the earth. To do so, place your feet or the palms of your hands flat on the ground. With each exhale, visualize and feel the excess energy draining from your body and into the earth. Keep this process going until you feel calm and balanced.

 ## EXERCISE 7:
Channeling External Power from Natural Sources

Purpose: To practice channeling external power from a natural source.

Location: A quiet, comfortable space.

Time: Anytime.

Tools: A natural object from which to channel power, such as a plant or stone.

To begin, close your eyes and take in a nice deep breath. Exhale, allowing your body and mind to still. If you are able to hold, touch, or otherwise physically feel the natural object, do so now. If you are unable to do so (such as when channeling power from planets), use your abilities of visualization to connect with your chosen power source. In either case, visualize that there is a swirling light within this object—this is its magical power. As in the previous exercise, the color of this light will vary by power source and their particular virtue.

Once you are able to see the magical power, visualize that with every inhale, the light from your chosen object gradually expands outward. Imagine the power forming waves, which proceed to wash over you. Feel the magic being absorbed into your body, through your skin, into your bloodstream, and merging with your own inner power. Picture how the color of the external power blends together with the color of your own. Notice how you feel with the added magical energy filling your body; hold this sensation for a minute or two.

Now, continuing to breathe steadily. Slowly let go of the external power. Imagine that the light of its magic is receding from your body and moving back toward its place of origin. Continue this process until the external power has left completely and you have returned to your normal state. As before, if needed, you can ground yourself by sending any excess energy into the earth to be recycled.

Projection

At this point, you have learned how to obtain the two necessary components for working effective magic—intention and power. Now, in order to complete the magical process, you must learn to fuse these components together and project them toward your desired outcome. When you project your combined intent and power, it can be sent to a visualized outcome or directly to a person, place, or situation. For example, you could send healing power to a sick friend, a hospital, or an influenza outbreak. Intent and power can also be projected into items such as charm-bags and candles. These items are commonly used as conduits for the magical power that can be stored within them and released steadily over time. In any case, you must simultaneously visualize your intention while raising or channeling power and then finally project them forth. Although this may sound difficult, it becomes easier the more you practice.

 EXERCISE 8:
Projecting Magical Power

Purpose: To practice projecting your conjoined intention and magical power.

Location: A quiet, comfortable space.

Time: Anytime.

Tools: A natural item, if channeling power from an external source.

Before you begin, decide on your magical intention. Then, start by visualizing this intention and the desired outcome in your mind's eye. Once the image is clear within your mind, momentarily shift your focus toward raising or channeling magical power. When the power starts to reach a climax, return focus to your intention. Finally, while holding a firm focus on your intention, visualize the power streaming forth from its source (internal or external) and toward its destination (e.g., a visualized outcome or a specific person, place, or object). At whatever point you feel that the projection of magical power is complete, allow your internal power to slow and release any channeled power—either back to its source or by grounding it into the earth.

Chapter 4

THE TRADITIONAL
WITCH'S TOOLS

When working magic, the most important tool for a Witch to have is their own mind. As seen in the previous chapter, the only essentials for magic are a clearly defined intention and the power necessary to make it manifest. Therefore, outside of any natural objects you may be channeling power from, you don't necessarily need any physical tools to work successful magic. However, physical tools can be immensely helpful for focusing and directing your magical power. Traditional Witchcraft is no different from any other magical path in that it incorporates a particular set of tools into its practice. Although, unlike those used in practices like ceremonial magic, the tools of Traditional Witchcraft tend to be quite utilitarian, serving both magical and mundane purposes. Be mindful that you don't inherently need every single tool listed in this chapter, nor do you need to rush out in order to find them. While these tools will be used in later exercises, in the true spirit of Traditional Witchcraft, you can always improvise or make do with what you have on hand.

Buying versus Making Tools

While collecting your magical tools, you have the option of either buying or making them by hand. When it comes to buying, there are many amazing artisans out there who sell an array of magical tools both in shops and online. Not only can you purchase beautifully created items, but you also have the chance to support the work of fellow Witches and other magical practitioners. Moreover, thrift stores and antique shops can be excellent places to find magical items. Some of my favorite magical tools were found in local antique shops, including a cast iron trivet with a pentagram in the center of its design. Whether you buy new or used, remember to take your time finding the right tools for your practice. Don't settle on something simply because it's available or because you're afraid that without it you won't be able to practice Traditional Witchcraft. Obtaining magical items in a hurry or out of anxiety often leads to the accumulation of objects that you have very little personal connection with and will likely never use. Having a deep connection with your tools is important because the more you resonate with them, the more attuned to your magic they will be. And, the more attuned to your magic the tools are, the more helpful they will be when you cast spells or perform rituals. While shopping, it may be helpful to ask yourself whether or not an item truly speaks to you and if or how it will benefit your practice. You might also ask yourself if the item is one you will use frequently or if it's something that will only gather dust before eventually being discarded.

On the other hand, you can also make your own tools. Doing so will naturally require more time and effort, but the results of your work will prove to be extremely rewarding. Through the actions and labor required to create a tool, you automatically infuse it with your magical power—a process which usually takes a longer amount of time with a tool that has been acquired from a store. There is an unbeatable sense of satisfaction and pride that comes along with the designing and producing of your own magical objects. Of course, there are some things you likely cannot make yourself (such as a cauldron, unless you know how to pour metal), but there are certain tools that are better off being made by your own hand. When making your tools, I encourage you to think creatively about what materials you might already have around the house or can find out in nature. Making tools, or buying for that matter, doesn't have to cost you an arm and a leg. There is no right or wrong way for a tool to look so long as it works for you. So be imaginative and don't be afraid to get your hands dirty. Crafting magical tools should feel like a fun ritualistic activity, not a burden or a chore.

The Stang

Throughout all of Traditional Witchcraft, the stang is one of the most iconic symbols of the Crooked Path. In its simplest of forms, the stang is a bifurcated ritual staff. The word *stang* is thought to come from the Old Norse *stöng*, meaning staff or pole. As a Witch's tool, its creation and implementation can be primarily credited to Robert Cochrane. Though you can spot forked branches being used by the Witches depicted in old artwork—such as those shown in Peter Binsfeld's *Tractatus de confessionibus maleficorum et sagarum* (1591)—before Cochrane, there are no mentions of a "stang" in connection with the Craft.

The Stang

In one of his letters to ceremonial magician William Gray, Cochrane referred to the stang as the supreme implement.[23] His statement rings true in that the stang is an incredibly multi-purpose tool, like the Swiss Army knife of Traditional Witchcraft. First and foremost, the stang is a representation of the Witch Father, the archetypal masculine deity with whom many Traditional Witches work, with the two tines of the staff being an homage to his horns. In this role, the stang is commonly placed at the northern point of the ritual space, which is the direction often associated with the Witch Father in folklore, although sometimes it will be planted in the center of the working area to be used as a magical focal point. In its capacity as an image of the Witch Father, the stang becomes an altar as well. As an altar, the stang may be adorned with different symbolic objects, such as a garland and crossed arrows, which signify the dual-aspect of the Witch Father as the light-bearing God of Life and the chthonic Lord of Death. Given the time of year, it may be decorated with seasonal foliage, like boughs of yew in the autumn and hawthorn in the spring. In addition, a lit taper candle can be placed between the tines as a sign of the *light betwixt the horns*, or the divine inspiration granted to us by the Witch Father. Finally, any other ritual or spell materials will be laid out at the base of the stang.

In a more operative function, the stang is similar to any other staff or wand in that it can also be used as a tool for directing magical power. The Traditional Witch projects their power out from their body and through the stang, and from the stang out into the universe. The stang can be used when laying a compass, calling up spirits, or casting spells. I personally like to hold on to mine while laying a compass as a means of focusing my power and as a general touchstone that

23. Robert Cochrane, "Letter Thirteen," in *The Robert Cochrane Letters: An Insight into Modern Traditional Witchcraft*, ed. Michael Howard (Somerset, UK: Capall Bann Publishing, 2002), 142.

transitions me into the ritual headspace. I also enjoy bringing it along with me when I go on hikes through the woods, allowing it to absorb some of the land's magical virtue to be used in later spellcraft.

The stang is one of those tools that is better off when made by the Witch's own hands, a process that can be done with relative ease and few materials. It is also a tool that allows for a lot of personal variation in terms of size and design. I have two stangs in my collection, both of which are handmade. The first is a simple wand-sized branch (approximately twelve inches long) that I painted black. The other one is a staff-length branch (approximately five feet tall) that is decorated with personal symbols and stained a dark brown.

 ## EXERCISE 9:
Creating a Stang

Purpose: To create your own stang.

Location: A workspace with a sturdy surface and proper ventilation.

Time: Anytime.

Tools: A forked branch, sandpaper, wood stain, paintbrush, paint (optional), and a wood burner (optional).

To begin, go out into a wooded area and search for a sturdy forked branch. You may find one that has already fallen from a tree or one that is still connected, in which case it will need to be cut using a small saw. Any type of wood will do, although ash is a traditional choice. If you're cutting a fresh branch, make sure to ask the spirit of the tree for permission first. If they agree, cut the branch evenly, doing as little damage to the tree as possible. Before leaving, no matter if your branch fell naturally or was cut, give thanks to the spirits with appropriate offerings, such as honey or milk. If the branch is fresh, allow it time to dry out before moving on to the next steps.

1. Strip the bark off the branch and sand it down until it's smooth.

2. Apply an even layer of stain.

3. If you wish, use a wood burner or paint to add symbols of personal power (e.g., pentagrams, runes, astrological signs, etc.).

Traditionally, the stang is finalized when it is shod with an iron nail, which is believed to ground its energy. If you'd like to do so, you can hammer a nail upward into the foot of the stang, but be careful, as this could cause the bottom to split.

The Cauldron

If the stang is a representation of the Witch Father, then the cauldron is a symbol for the Witch Mother, the archetypal feminine deity with whom many Traditional Witches work. The cauldron is commonly viewed as a feminine tool across magical traditions due to its ability to contain and transform material. Similar to the womb, the cauldron can take one thing (such as herbs and water) and create something else (like a medicinal tea). In this sense, the cauldron can be seen as an icon of the Generative Creatrix. From her depths, new life—in a variety of contexts both literal and metaphorical—emerges. Yet, at the same time, the cauldron can also be an emblem of the Weaver of Fate, the Veiled Lady or Crone who brings death upon us. In order for new things to emerge from the cauldron, they must first be sacrificed. And, when flipped upside down, this tool becomes reminiscent of the ancient burial mounds, a reminder that all things must die in order to be reborn.

The cauldron is frequently associated with the element of water, but it's also highly resonant with the element of fire. Many Traditional Witches will burn items in them, whether they be fragments of spells, incense, or actual miniature fires. Within the ritual space, a cauldron containing a small fire will commonly be placed in the center to act as a magical focal point. The cauldron has many additional utilitarian purposes. It can be used as a cooking vessel for food, drink, and medicine as well as for various spells. In magical working, the cauldron can be used to ritualistically give birth to a desired outcome. For example, you might place a poppet (a magical doll representing the target of a spell) inside the cauldron and then, at the end of the ritual, lift it out as a sign of the magic taking effect. Alternatively, the cauldron can be used for baneful magic. In this case, the cauldron could be placed upside down over a poppet as a way of entombing or containing an enemy.

There are many options for obtaining a cauldron. The traditional cast iron style is a popular choice because of its durability and the fact that it can withstand high levels of heat. Most occult suppliers carry cast-iron pots, but you can also buy them from specialty cooking and camping supply stores. Again, you may want to check out antique shops where you just might come across an old, used cauldron. In either case, you'll want to make sure that you season it in order to protect it from rusting. You can do this by coating the cauldron with a thin layer of olive oil and placing it upside down in an oven (at 375 degrees Fahrenheit) for about an hour. If the cauldron already has rust on it, an easy trick is to soak it in Coca-Cola overnight to loosen the rust and then scrub it away with steel wool in the morning.

There are cauldrons made out of other metals, including copper and brass. Or you may eschew the classical cauldron altogether and opt for a bowl or pot. I have a large ceramic bowl that I use for mixing herbs for spells and a terracotta flower pot I will use for lighting small fires. As always, it's up to your own creativity and personal preferences!

◊ FROM THE SPIRITS OF LORE: Medea's Cauldron

From the spirits of lore, there is a Greek story that gives an explanation for the different magical uses of cauldrons. As it goes, there once was a woman named Medea who was a Witch and a priestess to the goddess Hecate. She possessed great knowledge of *pharmaka*, or the use of herbs to make both medicines and poisons, which she would brew within her special cauldron. She used this knowledge and skill to help the hero Jason, whom she had fallen in love with, on his quest to retrieve the Golden Fleece (a symbol of his inheritance and the right to the throne). After successfully retrieving the Golden Fleece, Jason expressed to Medea his concerns regarding the health of his aged father, Aeson. In response, Medea performed a healing ritual in which she drained Aeson of his blood and replaced it with the juices of various herbs which she mixed together in her cauldron. As a result, the old man's health and vitality were restored.

Hearing of Medea's power, the daughters of King Pelias begged her to help them restore their father's health as she had done for Aeson. Unbeknownst to them, Pelias was an old enemy of Medea's, and she quickly concocted a deceptive scheme to dispatch of him. And so, she agreed to demonstrate her magical ritual to the daughters. She added special herbs to her cauldron before cutting the throat of an aged ram and then tossing it into the smoking pot. A moment or two later, the daughters were shocked to see a lamb spring forth from the cauldron. Of course, Medea, with her sly cunning, had given the daughters false instructions, and as a result, they unknowingly killed their own father when they performed the ritual.

Medea showed us the cauldron's power as a symbol of life and a tool for healing transformation when she used it to bring health back to Aeson. On the other hand, she also demonstrated how the cauldron can be a symbol of death and tool for destruction when she used it to trick Pelias's daughters into unwittingly murdering their father. While it's not recommended that you use your cauldron to the same harmful extent as Medea, her story attests to the fact that the cauldron can be used for a variety of magical functions both helpful and harmful.

The Broomstick

If there is another tool besides the cauldron as quintessential to the image of the Witch, it's the broomstick. Witches have been associated with brooms for centuries, with the popular belief being that they were used as a means of magical transportation. One of the earliest depictions of a Witch riding a broomstick appeared in 1451 as a marginal illustration in Martin le Franc's *Le champion des dames*. According to the notorious 1486 Witch-hunting manual, the *Malleus Maleficarum*, Witches would anoint their brooms with a special ointment and then be carried off into the air.[24]

While the broomstick isn't used for actual physical flight, it does serve as a useful tool in hedge-crossing. When used for this task, the Traditional Witch will lie outstretched and place the broom either alongside their body or under their knees, where it assists the spirit in Otherworldly travels. On a more mundane (but still magical) level, the broomstick is used for its original purpose, sweeping! The working space may be swept clean of both physical and energetic debris while simultaneously sweeping in that which the practitioner so desires. Therefore, the nature of the broom as a sweeper is twofold—to banish and to bless.

The broom is a tool that is quite easy to craft yourself, although there are plenty of artisans who make and sell gorgeous ones if you don't wish to create your own. While the classic materials for a Witch's broom are said to consist of

---

24. Heinrich Kramer and Jacbob Sprenger, *The Malleus Maleficarum*, trans. Montague Summers (1486; Mineola, NY: Dover Publications, 1971), 107.

an ash handle, birch brush, and willow bindings, it's important to use what is available and speaks to you.

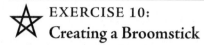

EXERCISE 10:
Creating a Broomstick

Purpose: To create your own broomstick.

Location: A workspace with a sturdy surface and proper ventilation.

Time: Anytime.

Tools: A straight branch, sandpaper, wood stain, a brush, 12 feet of sturdy cord (hemp or jute), and paint or a wood burner (optional).

To begin, go out to a wooded area and search for a sturdy branch to serve as the broom handle. If you're cutting a fresh branch, make sure to ask the land spirits for permission first. If they agree, cut the branch evenly, doing as little damage to the tree as possible. Before leaving, no matter if your branch was naturally fallen or cut, give thanks to the spirits with appropriate offerings, such as a small amount of honey or milk. If the branch is fresh, allow it time to dry out before moving on to the next steps.

1. Strip the bark off the branch and sand it down until it's smooth.
2. Apply an even layer of stain.
3. If you wish, use a wood burner or paint to add symbols of power to the handle.

Next, you will need to gather the brush for your broomstick. You might use thin, wispy brambles or perhaps the traditional broomcorn. Place the brush around the base of the broomstick handle and, with the sturdy cord, begin binding the brush to the handle. Start by wrapping the cord around the brush and handle once, pulling as tight as possible. Then make an initial knot, being sure to leave a length of cord to make the final knot at the end. Continue wrapping the cord tightly. When you near the end of the cord, tie the two ends together (using the length left over from the first knot) with a triple knot.

The Knife

For Traditional Witches, the knife is a tool of efficiency used for various tasks, such as carving candles and harvesting herbs. For these purposes, the blade should be sharp so as to make cutting easier. The knife is related to the powers of the Witch's mind, and therefore—in line with more ceremonial forms of magic—can be used for directing energy or working with spirits. It may even be used to delineate the boundaries of the compass by physically digging into the earth. By doing so, the knife acts as a microcosm of the larger ploughs used by farmers to work the land. In choosing, or making, your knife, you will want it to be sharp. Many blades that are available through occult suppliers have been dulled down and will need to be sharpened. New or used kitchen knives can work wonderfully and can be found relatively inexpensively at thrift or antique shops. In terms of specific style, the knife can be either single or double-edged, depending upon your own desires. Preferably the handle will be made of natural material like wood or bone. With those options, you will be able to carve, burn, or paint your personal symbols upon the hilt.

The Cup

The cup, like the cauldron, is commonly considered to be a tool of the Witch Mother. Its primary task is to hold liquids used in offertory rites to the spirits. As such, the cup is related to the mythical Holy Grail and the magical enlightenment it grants to those who partake from it. Out of all the tools, it is perhaps the cup that allows for the most variety in its design. There are the classic chalices, which can be made from ceramic, metal, stone, wood, or bone. Then there is the option of the drinking horn, which is quite popular among Traditional Witches. I have two cups that I alternate between, both ceramic (which is one of my favorite materials). One is a gorgeous chalice with an intricate pentacle design and the other is a modest coffee mug that was a gift from a good friend. Your tools don't have to be super flashy and fancy, unless of course that suits your style. They can be as simplistic as you'd like. It's about their meaning and functionality, not about how they might look or compare to someone else's.

The Dish

The dish is typically paired with the cup in offertory rites, used for holding offerings of food made to the spirits. It can also be used as a tool for charging, or *hallowing*, other objects, such as spell material. When used in this manner, the dish is left upon the altar or other special place to attract and absorb additional magical energy. For example, you might set a charm-bag on your dish and then leave them under the night sky to instill the bag with a certain planetary virtue. Comparable to the cup, there are many potential design choices for the dish. It could be an extravagant silver platter or a plain old dinner plate. The dish can be made from a variety of materials, including ceramic, stone, metal, and bone. One neat idea is to use the unglazed base of a terracotta flower pot, which you can buy separate from the pot in several different sizes and for pretty cheap. Any of these options may be enhanced by etching or painting magical characters upon their surface, such as a pentacle or certain runes. Your dish might not even be a dish at all—in the strictest sense of the word. The trivet I mentioned at the beginning of this chapter serves as my dish in addition to a copper bowl for loose offerings such as tobacco or herbs.

Candles and Incense

Candles and incense are magical staples for most Traditional Witches. Candles can be carved with symbols of intent and then hallowed with magical power. As the candle burns, the magic is released into the universe, where it will make manifest the Witch's desires. Incense works in a similar fashion, being infused with our intent and power and then burnt as a means of sending the magic to where it is needed. Candles and incense can also be used as offerings to the spirits. Both can be burnt while working magic with your spirit allies or when giving them thanks.

The type of candle used will depend upon personal preferences and the work at hand. If your magical working is meant to be ongoing or long term, you will want to use a larger candle that will have more burn time. If your working is meant to be quick or short term, you'll want to use a smaller candle, such as a votive, taper, chime, or tealight. Candles made from natural materials like beeswax, soy, and palm are preferable, as they burn cleaner and are better for the environment. However, these candles can be expensive and harder to obtain. Therefore, use what is available and what you can comfortably afford. The color of the candle will often be based upon your specific intention (e.g., green for prosperity, red for protection, blue for healing, etc.), but white and black candles work as great all-purpose magical options.

Incense comes in many forms, including the stick, cone, and loose varieties. Loose incense is often preferable because you are able to create your own blends with herbs, resins, and oils that specifically correspond to your magical intention. Loose incense can be burnt upon special charcoal discs in heat-safe containers, such as a cast-iron cauldron lined with an inch of sand. Stick and cone incense, on the other hand, are both easy to use and don't require as much prep work or setup. There are hundreds of incense brands out there that you can purchase from, with an infinite variety of scents. However, pay attention to the ingredients and watch out for synthetic fragrances and other harmful chemicals, which can be quite unpleasant to both you and the spirits.

Natural Items

Along with the tools just described, Traditional Witches use an assortment of natural items for rituals and spellcraft. By and large, these items can be placed into one of three different categories: the plant, stone, or animal kingdom. Common natural objects used by Traditional Witches are herbs, roots, rocks, fur, feathers, and bones. It's important that all these natural objects be respectfully and ethically sourced, meaning that you must adhere to local laws and refrain from taking anything that is legally forbidden. Additionally, make sure to remember that you ask the indwelling spirit of a natural object permission to take it with you and to respect if the spirit says no. We will focus more on natural tools and how to obtain them in chapter 11, but for now keep an eye out for things that could be useful, like a particular herb growing in the woods, a shiny piece of quartz at the bottom of a stream, or a couple of fallen bird feathers along a walking path. These are all things that could come in handy later on.

The Altar

The altar is a sacred place where Traditional Witches convene to work their spells and to commune with the spirits. The altar comes in many shapes and sizes, and there is no one correct way for it to look. It could be a coffee table, a shelf on the

wall, or cabinet which you can close when it's not in use. If you're lucky enough
to have a fireplace in your home (whether functional or not), the hearth makes a
fantastic altar. Chimneys are believed to be gateways through which spirits can
come to visit and spells can take flight. You may not even have a permanent altar, instead putting one together only when the need arises. There are outdoor
altars as well, which could be anything from a tree stump to a flat stone. Furthermore, the stang (as mentioned earlier) can be used as an altar by planting it in the
ground and arranging other magical items around its base.

As with all the other tools of Traditional Witchcraft, how you design your altar and how it functions is entirely up to you! Your altar can be cluttered, over-
flowing with your working tools, spell materials, and assorted natural items like
dried plants and bones. It could also be minimalistic, nice and neat with everything in a designated place. What matters the most is that it's arranged in a way
that is meaningful to you and your spirits and that it houses all the tools you'll
need to work your magic.

✪ EXERCISE 11:
Hallowing Ritual

Purpose: To hallow a new ritual tool, imbuing it with magical power.

Location: A quiet, comfortable space.

Time: The waxing or full moon.

Tools: A pillar candle (white or black in color), incense of your choosing, a tool to
be hallowed, a bowl of dirt, a bowl of water, and a disposable lancet (optional).

Light the candle and incense. Begin by passing the tool through the fragrant
incense smoke, saying aloud: *I hallow this (tool) by the primal powers of air and
wind.*

Next, pass the tool over the candle's flame, saying aloud: *I hallow this (tool) by
the primal powers of fire and flame.*

Then, dust the tool with a fine layer of dirt, saying aloud: *I hallow this (tool) by
the primal powers of earth and stone.*

Finally, sprinkle the tool with droplets of water, saying aloud: *I hallow this
(tool) by the primal powers of water and sea.*

Hold the tool in your hand and feel your own magic merging with the virtue already inherent within it. At this point, feed the tool by breathing upon it or rubbing it with a little of either your spit or your blood. Be safe! Use a sterile single-use diabetic lancet and wash your hands afterward. Inform the object of its intended purpose and sense as it comes alive to work your magical desires.

 ## FROM THE BLACK BOOK:
Hallowing Incense

To be used in all matters of blessing.

1 tablespoon ground frankincense resin

1 teaspoon sage leaf

1 teaspoon rosemary

1 teaspoon vervain

1 teaspoon mugwort

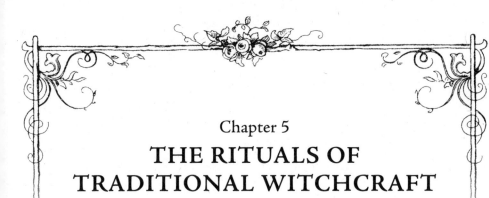

Chapter 5
THE RITUALS OF TRADITIONAL WITCHCRAFT

Ritual has many purposes within the practice of Traditional Witchcraft. When engaging in ritual, we are able to connect with the spirits, with the land, and with deeper parts of ourselves. Performing rituals allows us to communicate with the spirits, to honor, celebrate, and strengthen our relationships with these beings. Certain rituals even possess the ability to create a bridge between the natural world and the Otherworld, permitting the Witch entrance into the realms beyond. Operatively, ritual provides a means for working profound acts of magic. Through enchanted words and mysterious gestures, ritual provides a means of tapping into the currents of sorcerous power present within ourselves and within the world around us. Moreover, ritual helps amplify and direct these powers in a focused and intentional way.

While the rituals of the Crooked Path are widely varied, there are three that tend to be commonplace among the different permutations of Traditional Witchcraft. These three rituals —which can all be credited to Robert Cochrane—are known as the compass round, treading the mill, and the housel. Although they are relatively modern creations, each of these rituals is infused with elements of classical Witchcraft folklore, which lends them a sense of primordiality. Moreover, these three rituals stand out for being approachable and versatile while simultaneously complex and arcane. All at once they have the ability to empower, inspire, and mystify the Witches who perform them.

Simple, Ecstatic Ritual

The rituals performed by Traditional Witches tend to be ecstatic in nature, meaning they are spontaneous, wild, and emotional. Although the rituals described in this chapter follow a basic structure, that structure is only meant to be a foundation upon which personal improvisations can be added. A good ritual should promote a sense of connection, whether it's to the spirits or to magic in general. In order for there to be a connection, though, the actions and words contained in the ritual need to speak to you on a personal level. You can follow rituals that were written and laid out by other people, but if they don't elicit an emotional response within you, they're not likely to be very effective. When it comes to magic, if you don't resonate with the ritual on a deep level, then you end up merely going through the motions and the whole process falls flat. The use of pre-written rituals can be helpful practice for beginner Witches as they allow you to get a feel for how rituals are performed and what works best for you. But don't be afraid to break free from the mold and adapt material to align with your personal style at whatever point you feel ready.

Rituals can be as complex as you'd like, but in Traditional Witchcraft they gravitate toward being simple and to the point. There is a minimal use of tools, and those that are included in ritual are often practical, like candles and vessels for offerings. Actions performed are intuitive or even completely unscripted. For example, some of my most powerful rituals involved nothing more than stomping my feet on the ground and intoning nonsensical words that came straight from my own imagination. I've found that the spirits are much more receptive and the magic effective when you speak a few words from the heart versus droning on from a Latin chant you can't translate or even pronounce. For this reason, the Traditional Witch is much more likely to be found sitting by a bonfire under the full moon speaking plainly to the spirits than in a fancy ritual room reading from a long invocation. But truly, as long as you feel connected to a ritual, it doesn't matter if it entails an hour of complicated ritual or simply singing to the genius loci while dancing naked around a pine tree.

The Compass Round

In her book *An ABC of Witchcraft,* Doreen Valiente wrote that "the magic circle is part of the general heritage of magical practice, which is world-wide and of incalculable age."[25] Across different Witchcraft traditions, the use of ritually constructed circles is commonplace. How and why these circles are constructed vary between groups and individuals, yet they have always been a part of Witchcraft in one way or another. If you take a look through various depictions of Witches through the ages, you will uncover several that feature them dancing, feasting, and casting spells inside of a delineated circle. Additionally, many stone circles found throughout the world are linked to stories of Witchcraft and magic. Why are circles so popular amongst Witches—and other magical practitioners, for that matter? Magically speaking, the circle is a powerful shape because it symbolizes the cyclical nature of the world, including the stages of life, the changing of the seasons, and the movement of the planets. Additionally, circles allow for a better flow of power, as energy won't get stuck in corners as it would with any other shape. Like a whirlpool or tornado, within a circle you can generate more force due to the ease of cyclical movement.

Within the realm of Traditional Witchcraft, we make use of what is known as the *compass round*. On a fundamental level, the compass is a Witch's ritually constructed, circular-shaped, working space. It is an area that is mindfully set aside from the mundane, being designated for the working of magic and communing with the spirits. The compass is comparable to a semi-permeable membrane in that it works to keep out unwanted visitors (both physical and Otherworldly) while allowing only those who are welcome to cross through its barrier. Moreover, the compass contains the magical energy produced during ritual or spellwork until it's ready to be released. On a deeper level, though, and most central to Traditional Witchcraft, the compass is a liminal place, a doorway through which we can enter into the Otherworld. On one hand, the word *compass* is synonymous with the word *circle*, but it also denotes the well-known navigational tool used in travel. This second meaning makes a lot of sense in the context that Traditional Witches use the compass round to navigate and traverse the different realms.

In Traditional Witchcraft, we use the word *lay* to describe the ritual process for creating the compass round because, as a navigational tool, it is used for getting the lay of the land. In laying a compass round, Traditional Witches are formulating a magical map of the natural realm and the Otherworld. We call out to the spirits

---

25. Doreen Valiente, *An ABC of Witchcraft* (Custer, WA: Phoenix Publishing, 1973), 64.

of the four directions—north, south, east, and west—as well as the spirits of the above and below. We invite them to join our compass round and in turn, the roadways that lead into their realms are opened. The compass then becomes a six-way crossroads, in the center of which the powers of the natural world and the Otherworld converge. The Traditional Witch, in spirit form, can walk the roadways into the realms beyond or remain at the midpoint in physical body—taking advantage of the confluence of powers—in order to work acts of magic.

When calling to the spirits of the four directions, it's not unusual for Traditional Witches—like other magical practitioners—to ascribe them with particular elemental virtues (e.g., earth, air, fire, and water). These elemental virtues are useful in that they exist as the energetic building blocks of both the natural world and the Otherworld. Therefore, calling upon the elements is a way of bringing the two worlds together within the compass round. While each of the elements can be found in all directions, by using physical landmarks as specific points of reference, you can better organize their magical power. In order for this to be effective, though, the elements need to be assigned to directions that make sense in your given landscape. For example, where I live, I assign air to the north because it is from this direction that the strongest wind blows. Earth is placed in the south, as this is where my favorite expanse of woods is located. Fire is assigned to the east due to the rising sun, while water is placed in the west, where a large body of water can be found. Pay attention to your local landscape when determining which elements go where and experiment with different alignments until you find one that works.

Let's take a moment to look at how Robert Cochrane described his layout of the compass round. In his ritual, the Witch creates three concentric rings—sometimes referred to as "moats" as they were physically dug into the ground—around a fixed point, such as a cauldron filled with fire. The rings are created from the outside, moving inward, as each one represents a different stage in the life cycle that must be crossed in order to reach the Otherworld. The first ring is made of salt, which stands for life; the second is made from ash (traditionally that of birch and willow wood), which stands for death and rebirth; and the third is made from a mixture of water, wine, vinegar, and sugar, which stands for the river that is crossed into the Otherworld. In the very center of the space lies what he called the "Castle," or the place where the four directions meet. It is here where magic is wrought and the Witch meets with the spirits.[26]

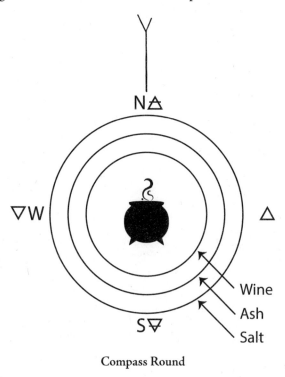

Compass Round

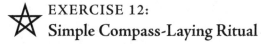 **EXERCISE 12:**
Simple Compass-Laying Ritual

Purpose: To practice a simple method for laying a compass round.

Location: Outdoors or indoors.

   Time: Anytime.

Tools: Incense, a pillar candle (white or black in color), a bowl of dirt, a bowl of water, and your stang.

Begin by circling your working space (starting in the north, the direction of the Witch Father) with the burning incense, allowing the smoke to waft freely and envisioning the powers of air permeating the atmosphere. Next, circle the

---

26. Cochrane, "Letter Thirteen," in *The Robert Cochrane Letters*, 139–41.

space with the lit candle, feeling the powers of fire blazing all around. Then, dust a fine layer of dirt around the circumference, picturing the powers of earth emerging up from the ground. Finally, making your last round, sprinkle droplets of water, sensing the powers of water flowing about the space.

Returning to the north, stand with stang in hand and say aloud: *I call to the spirits of the north, the primal powers of air and wind. I ask that you lend your virtues to my working and join my compass round.*

Move to the east and say: *I call to the spirits of the east, the primal powers of fire and flame. I ask that you lend your virtues to my working and join my compass round.*

Move to the south and say: *I call to the spirits of the south, the primal powers of earth and stone. I ask that you lend your virtues to my working and join my compass round.*

Move to the west and say: *I call to the spirits of the west, the primal powers of water and sea. I ask that you lend your virtues to my working and join my compass round.*

Standing once more in the north, plant the stang into the ground (if you are working indoors, set the stang against the northern wall or plant it in a flower pot filled with soil) and say: *I call to the Witch Father and Witch Mother, I call to the spirits of the land and the spirits of my ancestors. I ask that you lend your virtues to my working and join my compass round.*

When you wish to dismantle the compass, walk the circumference of the space counterclockwise, starting in the north. As you walk, speak your words of gratitude and farewell to each of the directions as well as to the Witch Father and Witch Mother, spirits of the land, and your ancestors. Finish by pulling the stang up from the ground and cleaning your working space.

 ## EXERCISE 13:
Cochrane-Inspired Compass-Laying Ritual

Purpose: To practice a Cochrane-inspired method for laying a compass round.

Location: A large outdoor area.

Time: Anytime.

Tools: Your stang; a bowl of salt; a bowl of ash; a container filled with a mixture of 1 cup water, 1 cup wine (or grape juice), 1 cup vinegar, and 1 cup sugar; and 4 pillar candles (white or black in color).

Before you begin, plant the stang in the ground (in the center of your working space), and then walk backward ten feet. You will be counting your footsteps in order to keep track of the rings which you are about to make. With the salt, walk around clockwise, forming the first ring (it doesn't need to be more than a sprinkle of salt). Once you've returned to your starting point, step over the line, entering the circle while saying aloud: *I cross this ring and move through the world of the living.*

Next, step forward two feet and form the second ring made of ash (again, it needn't be more than a sprinkle of ash). When complete, step over the line, entering the second circle while saying: *I move from life and into death.*

Then, step forward another two feet and form the third ring made from the mixture of water, wine, vinegar, and sugar. When complete, step over the line, entering the third and final circle, saying: *I cross the river and into the Otherworld.*

Place the four candles at the different points of the compass, moving clockwise from north to west. As you light each candle, call out to the spirits of each direction, asking them to join your compass round. Finally, stand in the center and call upon the Witch Father and Witch Mother or other spirits of your choosing.

When you wish to dismantle the compass, walk the circumference of the space counterclockwise starting in the north, saying thanks to the spirits and extinguishing the candles. Do the same for the Witch Father and Witch Mother (or other spirits you have called upon) before uprooting the stang. Proceed to walk four feet from the center toward the third ring and step over into the second circle, saying: *I cross over the river and out of the Otherworld.*

Walk another two feet toward the second ring and cross over into the first circle, saying: *I move out of death and back into life.* Finally, walk two more feet and step out of the first ring, effectively dismantling the compass round.

Treading the Mill

Treading the mill is a ritual used to alter consciousness and to raise personal magical power. It involves continual pacing, or treading, about the compass round while maintaining a fixed gaze upon a central point of reference, such as a bonfire or stang. Although treading the mill is a relatively modern invention, it contains echoes of the ring dances reputedly used by Witches of the past. Throughout trial records there are accounts of Witches dancing in rings around central objects, such as Margaret Og, who was said to have danced around a giant stone with her coven on Hallowmas, or those at Aberdeen, who danced around the market cross.[27] The name of the ritual itself refers to the old-fashioned mills which work in a circular fashion to grind grains—again connecting Witches with the working of the land. The mill can be viewed as a metaphor for the way that the Witch paces the compass in order to grind out, or raise the magical power necessary to obtain a desired outcome. The direction in which the mill is trod depends upon the magical intention for which the power is being raised. A clockwise direction is used for beneficent workings and a counterclockwise for baneful ones.

When treading the mill, the Witch moves forward with their head turned to the side and slightly cocked back, gazing steadily upon the central point. By walking with your head turned to the side and slightly tilted back, you effectively restrict some of the blood flow to your brain. When this is paired with the continuous focus upon a central point, it creates a hypnotic effect. In this way, treading the mill acts as a means of inducing the trancelike state that is vital for working magic. Traditionally, the mill is trod with slow and steady movement, sometimes with one foot dragging behind the other—an action known as the lame step (an homage to the lame-footed spirits of blacksmithing, such as Tubal Cain, who were venerated by Cochrane). However, the mill can also be trod with gaining intensity, transforming into a frenzied dance around the compass. When you move with gathering speed, your heart begins to beat faster, your blood quickens, and your power starts to move within your body. Whether you tread the mill fast or slow, you will fall into a trance and power will be amassed—typically culminating in an energetic climax during which you make a sudden stop, causing a release of magical shockwaves. You might throw your hands up and project these waves of power toward a magical intention, or you may fall to the ground, riding them into a deeper trance wherein communication with spirits commonly occurs.

---

27. Thomas Davidson, *Rowan Tree & Red Thread* (Edinburgh, UK: Oliver and Boyd, 1949), 18.

⛤ EXERCISE 14:
Treading the Mill Ritual

Purpose: To practice treading the mill.

Location: A large outdoor area.

Time: Anytime.

Tools: Compass-laying tools (pillar candle, a bowl of water, a bowl of dirt, incense, and your stang) and a focal object (e.g., stang, bonfire, pillar candle, stone).

Begin by laying a compass using the Simple Compass-Laying Ritual on page 61 and then placing your focal object in the center of the space. Then, proceed to walk the circumference of the compass, starting in the north and moving either clockwise or counterclockwise, depending upon your magical intention. Look to your side, cocking your head back so that your chin touches your shoulder. Fix your gaze upon your focal object and keep walking. When you feel ready, begin the following chant:

> *Round about the mill I tread,*
> *Pointed finger, crooked head.*
> *Round about the mill I dance,*
> *Magic power, Witch's trance.*
> *Round about the mill I sing,*
> *Wishes grant, desires bring!*

With each circling of the compass, you might gain momentum and speed—repeating the chant with increasing fervor. Or you may retain a steady pace, perhaps making use of the lame step. Feel the power rising within you, flowing from your body and filling the space. When you sense that the magic is reaching a climax, when the air is crackling and your skin feels electrified, repeat the chant one last time. On the final note, either make a sudden stop and throw up your hands or fall to the ground if you are able. With that last gesture, feel the magic being released, sent forth to fulfill your desires.

When you've finished treading the mill and wish to dismantle the compass, walk the circumference of the space counterclockwise, starting in the north. As you walk, speak your words of gratitude and farewell to each of the directions as well as to the Witch Father and Witch Mother, spirits of the land, and your ancestors. Finish by pulling the stang up from the ground and cleaning your working space.

The Housel

The housel is a ritual of communion and thanksgiving during which the spirits are offered both food and drink. The word *housel* comes from the Old English *hūsl*, which originally meant sacrifice or offering but later came to be used as another term of the Christian Eucharist ceremony. Hearkening back to folklore, ritual feasting was one of the integral parts in the stories told about the Witches' Sabbath. The accused Witches of Salem were said to have feasted upon red bread and red wine at their meetings with the Devil.[28] Meanwhile, accused Scottish Witch Isobel Gowdie confessed that her coven would go around to several houses at night, sneaking inside and consuming the resident's entire store of food. Before their meal, though, the Witches would pray to the Devil, who sat at the head of the table:

> We eat this meat in the Divellis nam,
> With sorrow, and sych, and meikle shame;
> We sall destroy hows and hald;
> Both sheip and noat in till the fald.
> Litle good sall come to the fore
> Of all the rest of the little store![29]

Invoking a certain amount of atavism, Traditional Witches continue the legacy of ritual feasting when performing the housel. Similar to the Witches of folklore, the housel is enacted as a way of fortifying our relationship with the spirits. Whether they have helped us with spellwork or provided insight and guidance on a certain matter, we share food and drink as a sign of our gratitude for all that they have done for us. At the same time, we participate in the ritual meal, eating and drinking as a means of accepting the blessings of our spirits. Together,

28. Bryan F. Le Beau, *The Story of the Salem Witch Trials* (New York: Routledge, 2016), 99.

29. Robert Pitcairn, *Ancient Criminal Trials in Scotland*, vol. 3, pt. 2 (Edinburgh, UK: Bannatyne Club, 1833), 612, https://books.google.com/books?id=9tdLAAAAYAAJ.

Witches and spirits partake in the meal—sometimes while conversing lively and at other times while in silent communion. I have experienced housel rituals that have been sprightly and others that have been quite somber (this seems to depend on the time of year, with the former occurring in the summer and spring, while the latter tend to be in the autumn and winter).

As part of a larger ritual, the housel is usually performed toward the end as a way of thanking the spirits for attending and lending their virtues to the working. The housel can also be performed as its own standalone rite whenever you so wish. The food and drink used as offerings will be contingent upon the spirits you work with, as they usually have their own particular tastes and preferences (different types of offerings will be discussed in chapter 8). However, for the housel, an offering of wine, cider, or juice is typically paired with bread or cakes.

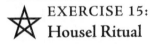

EXERCISE 15:
Housel Ritual

Purpose: To practice the housel ritual.

Location: Indoors or outdoors.

Time: Anytime.

Tools: Your cup filled with wine (or juice) and your dish containing a small loaf of bread.

To begin, hold your hand above your cup and make the sign of an equal-armed cross three times, saying aloud: *I bless this wine/juice in the name of the Witch Father and Witch Mother, in the name of the spirits of the land and the spirits of my ancestors.*

Next, hold your hand above your dish and repeat the gestures, saying: *I bless this bread in the name of the Witch Father and Witch Mother, in the name of the spirits of the land and the spirits of my ancestors.*

Now lift both the cup and the dish to the sky and say: *I offer this wine/juice and bread to the spirits as a token of my gratitude. As we partake in this meal, I honor and strengthen my connection to you, the Old Ones.*

Commence the ritual feast, eating and drinking while communing and giving thanks to your spirits. Split the bread, leaving half upon the dish for the spirits and eating the remainder. If working outdoors, pour half the wine/juice upon the ground; otherwise, drink your half and leave the rest for the spirits. After the ritual has ended, leave the bread and wine upon your altar overnight before disposing of it (either tossing it in the trash or composting it) in the morning.

 ### FROM THE BLACK BOOK:
Sabbath Bread

1¼ cups boiling water

1 cup oats

½ cup butter

1½ cups honey

2 eggs

1 teaspoon vanilla extract

1¾ cups flour

1 teaspoon baking soda

¾ teaspoon salt

1 teaspoon cinnamon

¼ teaspoon nutmeg

¼ teaspoon ground ginger

Preheat the oven to 350 degrees Fahrenheit. In a bowl, pour the boiling water over the oats and butter. Cover the bowl with a paper towel and let stand for 20 minutes. Meanwhile, mix together the honey, eggs, and vanilla in a separate container. Next, add in the oat and butter mixture, flour, baking soda, salt, and spices. Place the dough in a well-greased bread pan and put it in the oven for approximately 30 to 40 minutes.

EXERCISE 16:
Ritual Reflection

Purpose: To reflect upon your experiences performing the rituals in this chapter.

Location: A quiet space where you can think and write.

Time: Anytime.

Tools: Your journal and a pen.

In your journal, respond to the following questions:

+ What was it like preparing for the ritual? What tools did you use?
+ Did the ritual take place inside or outside? What effect do you think that had on the outcome?
+ How did you feel while performing the ritual? Were you nervous, excited, happy?
+ What was the best part of the experience for you?
+ What could have gone better? What do you think you'd do differently next time?

Chapter 6

SPELLCRAFT

Traditional Witches cast spells and craft charms. We mix herbs, carve candles, tie knots, and whisper words of enchantment, all in order to affect the world around us. We are agents of change, whether it be big or small. With our skills of spellcraft, we are able to use our magic to sway the very hand of fate. The Traditional Witch employs spells and charms for an assortment of reasons, including increasing luck, attracting love, generating healing, and promoting protection. Given the dual nature of Traditional Witchcraft, we also use our magic to banish, hex, and curse when the situation calls for it. The spells and charms used by Traditional Witches are often adapted from folklore, reworked and revitalized to meet present-day needs. They are also exceptionally pragmatic, involving everyday items that can be found around the house, in the kitchen, or from the garden. While some instructions or recipes may call for hard-to-obtain objects or ingredients, the Traditional Witch knows how to substitute and replace them when necessary. After all, the Traditional Witch's approach to spellcraft is one that is creative, cunning, and utilitarian.

High and Low Magic

In occult theory, magic is typically divided into two separate categories, high and low. Not to be mistaken as a judgment regarding the intrinsic worth of these approaches, *high* and *low* simply refer to the ways in which the magic is worked—specifically the sources from which power is drawn. High magic is ceremonial in nature, characterized by long, elaborate rituals that require a number of specific tools. Practitioners of high magic typically invoke spirits such as angels or demons in order to work their will (think of high magic as being heavenly or celestial). Historically, those who practiced high magic were more likely to be part of the upper class or at least somewhat affluent. They would have needed to have higher rates of literacy in order to read grimoires and a decent amount of money to obtain the necessary ritual equipment. Meanwhile, low magic was more common among the lower class, whose needs were more related to the everyday essentials of life—income, food, shelter, and protection. Low magic is down to earth and practical, focusing on partnering with the powers of the natural world so as to manifest one's desires (think of low magic as being earthy or natural). Don't be fooled, though—the line that separates high and low magic is not a definite one. Instead, the two exist on more of a continuum, with plenty of shades in the middle where they intermingle. A great historical example of the thin line between high and low magic can be seen in the practices of the Cunning Folk, who would regularly take elements of high magic—obtained through any magical texts that they could get a hold of—and would alter them to meet the needs of the average person.

In Traditional Witchcraft, you will find practitioners utilizing both high and low magic. There are individuals and groups whose practices are quite ceremonial, following classical grimoires, or books of magic, such as the Key of Solomon or the Book of Abramelin. There are also more modern grimoire systems, such as those written by the late Andrew Chumbley, that lay out an entire tradition in themselves. Conversely, many Traditional Witches have a proclivity for low magic, eschewing the scripts and props for the ecstatic gestures and verse used in the rituals described in the previous chapter. It's not to say that magical implements and pre-written spells aren't powerful or meaningful but rather that sometimes we run the risk of becoming a little too caught up in the physical trappings. It's not an uncommon experience for a Witch to become overly concerned with what tools, ingredients, or words they believe are necessary for a working. While it's always a good idea to thoroughly think through and prepare for magical undertakings, if it's gotten to the point where you're filled with anxiety over what color candle to use or if your spell is written in perfect iambic pentameter, then you may want to slow down and take a couple of breaths. Remember, it's all about what meaning it has to you, what is readily available, and what gets results, whether that involves you raising demons with flashy swords and thuribles or singing a song while tying knots in a cord under the waxing moon.

Adapting Spells and Charms from Folklore

Given that we are immensely inspired by folklore, Traditional Witches habitually take a gander into the past to find examples of spells and charms. In this instance, the Traditional Witch may utilize something verbatim, such as a prayer or invocation that has been tried and true throughout the ages. However, we are still likely to update it in order to make it more useful to our modern era, which is beside the fact that many spells and charms have already been altered significantly as they've exchanged hands over time. An example of this can be seen in regard to what is known as the Second Merseburg Charm. Originally discovered in 1841, the Merseburg charms are two incantations originally written in Old High German sometime in the ninth or tenth century. The second charm was traditionally used for the healing of injuries suffered by horses, specifically sprained legs:

> *Phol and Wodan went to the forest.*
> *Then Balder's horse sprained its foot.*
> *Then Sinthgunt sang charms, and Sunna her sister;*
> *Then Friia sang charms, and Volla her sister;*
> *Then Wodan sang charms, as well he could:*
> *be it bone-sprain, be it blood-sprain, be it limb-sprain:*
> *bone to bone, blood to blood,*
> *limb to limb, so be they glued together.*[30]

Today, the Second Merseburg Charm exists in many variations, all of which retain its original pattern but update the language and widen its use for different ailments (both animal and human). For example, a modern version that is much shorter and simpler goes like this:

> *This is the spell that I intone,*
> *Flesh to flesh and bone to bone,*
> *Sinew to sinew and vein to vein,*
> *And each one shall be whole again.*[31]

---

30. John Lindow, *Norse Mythology: A Guide to Gods, Heroes, Rituals, and Beliefs* (New York: Oxford University Press, 2001), 227–28.

31. Graham King, *The British Book of Spells and Charms* (London: Troy Books, 2014), 112.

There are thousands upon thousands of spells and charms out there, from countless regions and time periods. Examples of old folk magic can sometimes be found in modern spellbooks; however, you are more likely to find them in books specifically dedicated to the topic of folklore. Keep in mind, though, that no matter how old a spell or charm may be, it's only going to be powerful if it's meaningful to you. If the spell you're looking to cast or the charm you're looking to create calls for a rare root you've never heard of or the heart of a dove and you're uncomfortable using animal parts, you will need to either find a substitute or a different spell or charm altogether. Remember to be clever and crafty when working magic. Know your limits and don't be afraid to adapt spells and charms to better suit your personal needs and skill level.

 EXERCISE 17:
Adaptation of Folkloric Spells and Charms

Purpose: To practice adapting folkloric spells and charms to fit the context of your life.

Location: A quiet space where you can think and write.

Time: Anytime.

Tools: Your journal and a pen.

Begin by looking for examples of folk magic, either in books or on the internet. Once you've found a spell or charm that speaks to you, copy it into your journal and then answer the following questions:

+ What is the origin of this spell or charm? What culture or region does it come from?
+ What do you find useful about this particular spell or charm?
+ What parts of the spell or charm could use updating? Is there working that could be changed? An ingredient that could be added, subtracted, or substituted?
+ What ways can you rework the spell or charm to fit your specific needs?

Amulets and Charm-Bags

Along with verbal spells, Traditional Witches work with physical objects that inherently contain magical virtue or are otherwise imbued with power. These objects are known as amulets, talismans, and—in a second sense of the word—charms. There is some debate over how these three terms compare to one another, but for our purposes we will focus on them as items used to promote one's magical intention. Familiar examples include such things as horseshoes, four-leaf clovers, hagstones, rabbit's feet, and mercury dimes. Furthermore, assorted natural materials are frequently combined to fashion charm-bags. Folklorist William Bottrell described how the Cunning Folk would regularly give clients cloth bags containing earth, teeth, bones, and scraps of paper with magical words written upon them.[32] Today, Traditional Witches (among many other magical practitioners) continue this custom by making charm-bags with herbs, stones, and other items whose virtues correspond with their specific intention. Pieces of paper featuring spells, prayers, and magical symbols—including psalms, planetary squares, and pentacles—may also be added to these bags for extra power.

EXERCISE 18:
Creating a Charm-Bag for Luck

Purpose: To practice creating a charm-bag intended to incur luck.

Location: A quiet space with a sturdy work surface.

Time: Thursday during a waxing moon.

Tools: Dried mint leaves, cloves, and orange peel; 3 pennies or a piece of pyrite; a square of cotton cloth (white or green in color); and a length of cord. Optionally, you might wish to add a copy of the planetary square of Jupiter (see page 182).

Begin by mixing the three herbs, speaking words of intention as you blend them together. Next, breathe three times upon the coins or pyrite, focusing on your desire for good fortune. If using the square of Jupiter, fold the paper in half,

---

32. William Bottrell, *Traditions and Hearthside Stories of West Cornwall*, vol. 1 (Penzance, UK: W. Cornish, 1870), electronic reproduction by John Bruno Hare for the Internet Sacred Text Archive, 116, https://www.sacred-texts.com/neu/celt/swc1/index.htm.

making sure to fold toward yourself—which brings luck your way. Lay all three components upon the cloth and then bind it together with the cord. Hold the finished charm-bag in your hands and breathe three more times upon it, feeling the inherent virtues of its contents combining with your own magical power in order to fulfill your desires.

The charm-bag can be worn around your neck, carried in your pocket, or left in a special place, such as upon your altar.

FROM THE BLACK BOOK: Additional Charm-Bag Recipes

You can create additional charm-bags using the following recipes and adjusting the instructions from exercise 18 to fit the specific magical intention (e.g., protection, love, healing, and intuition).

Protection: A square of cotton cloth (white or red in color), a length of cord, a piece of obsidian, dried rosemary, thistle, and black peppercorns. Optionally, you might wish to add a copy of the planetary square of Mars (see page 182).

Love: A square of cotton cloth (white or pink in color), a length of cord, a heart-shaped or pink-colored stone, dried rose petals, yarrow, and catnip. Optionally, you might wish to add a copy of the planetary square of Venus (see page 182).

Healing: A square of cotton cloth (white or blue in color), a length of cord, a piece of seaglass, dried chamomile, plantain, and blue vervain. Optionally, you might wish to add a copy of the planetary square of the sun (see page 183).

Intuition: A square of cotton cloth (white or purple in color), a length of cord, a piece of natural quartz, mullein, wormwood, and mugwort. Optionally, you might wish to add a copy of the planetary square of the moon (see page 181).

Witch Bottles

Witch bottles are an excellent example of an old folk magic custom that has evolved over time. Classically speaking, the Witch bottle was a device used to counteract all manner of baneful magic. Recorded instructions for creating a Witch bottle advised one to "stop the urine of the Patient close up in a Bottle, and put into it three Nails, Pins, or Needles, with a little white Salt, keeping the urine always warm."[33] The magical theory behind the bottle is that it acts as a representation of the ill-wisher's bladder. The cork prevents them from passing urine while the pins cause them great pain, which would be exacerbated by the bottle being placed on a fire. It is thought that the guilty person would become so anguished that they would be forced to reverse their hex. Witch bottles have also been found hidden in the walls of old homes and buried beneath hearths and front doorstep. It may be that the bottles were also used as a general protective measure. An individual's urine (bottles have also been found containing hair and nail clippings), as an extension of oneself, can act as a magical decoy. Any maleficence sent toward the individual would be drawn to the bottle, wherein it would become stuck by the pins, essentially destroying the negative energy. Today, many practitioners continue to make use of Witch bottles, although more often in the latter sense described.

FROM THE SPIRITS OF LORE:
The Toothakers' Witch Bottle

From the spirits of lore, there is an American story that demonstrates the original use and method for creating a Witch bottle. As it goes, there once was a Massachusetts man named Roger Toothaker who was arrested on May 18, 1692, on charges of Witchcraft.[34] Toothaker was a local physician who was known to specialize in folk healing and appeared to have had some knowledge of working with herbs, astrology, and magic. While there is not much known about his trial due to a lack of written records, it is known that his wife and daughter were also accused of Witchcraft. His wife, Mary, confessed to having made a pact with the Devil, who appeared to her in the form of a "tawny man." She explained that in exchange for protection from the invading Indians, she had signed her name in blood upon a piece of birch bark.[35]

---

33. John Brand, *Observations on Popular Antiquities* (London: Chatto and Windus, 1877), 602, https://catalog.hathitrust.org/Record/102427510.

34. K. David Goss, *Documents of the Salem Witch Trials* (Santa Barbara, CA: ABC-CLIO, 2018), 63.

35. Juliet Haines Mofford, *The Devil Made Me Do It!: Crime and Punishment in Early New England* (Guilford, CT: Globe Pequot Press, 2012), 128.

One of the existing documents regarding Roger Toothaker's trial is a testimony given by a man named Thomas Gage.[36] According to his account, Gage had once heard Toothaker boasting about how his daughter, Margaret, had killed a local Witch. When asked how she had accomplished such a feat, Toothaker haughtily explained that he had taught his daughter a special technique. He elaborated that when someone had been bewitched, you were to take their urine and seal it in a bottle. The bottle of urine was then to be placed in a hot oven and left overnight. He claimed that by morning, the Witch would be dead and whatever evil magic she had done would be nullified.

 EXERCISE 19:
Creating a Protective Witch Bottle

Purpose: To practice creating a Witch bottle for matters of protection.

Location: A quiet space with a sturdy work surface.

Time: Tuesday during the waning moon, or on the night of a new moon.

Tools: A glass jar with a screw-on lid; a cup of salt; three pins, needles, or nails; and enough of your own urine to fill the jar. For added strength, you can add your nail clippings and a few strands of hair.

Begin by filling the jar with the salt. If using hair and nail clippings, add them next. Hold the three pins, needles, or nails in your hand and focus on your intention of dismantling harmful forces before dropping them into the jar. Finally, fill the rest of container with your urine. Screw the lid on tight and give the whole thing a good shake, envisioning all ill will being redirected into the jar and thoroughly destroyed.

The Witch bottle can be buried near your front door or otherwise hidden somewhere within your home. I recommend replacing the bottle every three months with one freshly created. Use a new jar each time and dispose of the old one in the trash.

Witch's Ladders and Knotted Cords

The Witch's ladder is a mysterious piece of folk magic whose exact purpose and provenance remains unknown. The ladder is essentially a length of cord tied with

---

36. Goss, *Documents of the Salem Witch Trials*, 66–67.

knots and bird feathers. The first mention of a Witch's ladder appeared in an article published in *The Folk-lore Journal* during 1887.[37] The article detailed how the ladder had been discovered, approximately ten years earlier, in the roof of a house that was being demolished. The author mentioned that he had seen the object firsthand and that the workers who were tearing down the house explained to him that it was a ladder that enabled Witches to cross from one rooftop to another. Over time, this enchanted cord has been variously thought to allow practitioners to steal milk from their neighbors' cows and to cause death to their enemies.[38]

While we may never know the intended use for that original Witch's ladder, we do know that there is a long history of Witches using knotted cords in their spellcraft. Witches from the Isle of Man were said to sell sailors cords that had been knotted with favorable winds.[39] When they were in need, they only had to undo a knot for the wind to fill their sails. Cords were also featured in many folk spells for healing, such as one in which a string with nine knots was to be tied around a child's neck to cure them of whooping cough.[40] In order to protect oneself from a hex, or to reverse the effects of one, a knotted red thread was to be worn around the neck and used like a rosary, with charms being spoken for each knot.[41] Today, Witch's ladders are created for just about any purpose, including both healing and protection. Spells are cast by tying a number of knots—usually in sets of three, nine, or thirteen—along a cord, concentrating each with magical power. For added strength, feathers, beads, bones, pins, keys, and hagstones are frequently strung along the cord as well.

EXERCISE 20:
Creating a Witch's Ladder

Purpose: To practice creating a Witch's ladder to help fulfill a magical intention of your choosing.

---

37. Valiente, *An ABC of Witchcraft*, 398–400.

38. Valiente, *An ABC of Witchcraft*, 398–400.

39. Arthur William Moore, *The Folk-Lore of the Isle of Man* (London: Brown & Son, 1891), 76.

40. John Harland and Thomas Turner Wilkinson, *Lancashire Folklore* (London: Frederick Warne and Co., 1867), 75, https://archive.org/details/lancashirefolklo00harl/page/n4.

41. F. Marian McNeill, *The Silver Bough* (Edinburgh, UK: Canongnate Publishing, 1989), 165.

Location: A quiet space with a sturdy work surface.

Time: Any time that corresponds with your intention (see chapter 12 for more information on favorable times for different magical workings).

Tools: A length of cord measuring about 30 inches in length (in a color that suits your specific intention) and nine bird feathers.

Once you've decided on the specific purpose of your ladder, start by folding the cord in half, bringing the two ends together. Create a loop and slowly begin to pull as if you were going to tie a knot in the center of the cord. But before you complete the knot, speak words of intention and place the end of a feather into the loop. When you feel the power pass into the cord, pull the ends and complete the knot. Repeat this process of tying knots and projecting power, alternating from left to right along the cord, for a total of nine knots.

When you're finished, hold the ladder in your hands and feel its power awakening to manifest your desires. You may hang the ladder in some secret place or leave it upon your altar. At any point, to strengthen the spell, you may touch each knot individually, repeating your words of intention as you go along.

Poppets and Image Magic

One form of spellcraft that is quite prevalent throughout the folklore of Witchcraft involves what is known as *image magic*. Although image magic can be utilized for a plethora of reasons, it has historically been a popular means of working baneful magic. By this technique, the Witch creates and works upon a doll—commonly known as a *poppet*—or some other representation of their intended victim. The image acts as a sort of focal point through which the target can then be affected by the spell. Isobel Gowdie and her coven used clay figures on several occasions to work baneful magic on their enemies. To do so, they would periodically stick the dolls with pins and roast them over a fire. To further their malefic power, the Witches would use the following incantation:

> *In the Divellis nam, we powr in this water among this mowld (meall,)*
> *For lang duyning and ill heal;*
> *We putt it into the fyre,*
> *That it mey be brunt both stik and stowre.*

It salbe brunt, with owr will,
As any stikle wpon a kill.[42]

Representations of victims can be constructed out of clay, wax, cloth, or other media. To strengthen the connection between the victim and the image, personal effects such as hair, fingernails, a scrap of clothing, or even a sample of their handwriting are added to it. In order to obtain one of these items, you'll need to be sneaky. But if you truly cannot get your hands on any personal effects, using a picture of the target can work just as well. The Witch will then baptize the representation with the victim's name, breathing life into it and establishing the bond between it and the victim.

 ## EXERCISE 21:
Creating a Poppet for Hexing

Purpose: To practice creating a poppet for hexing an enemy.

Location: A quiet space with a sturdy work surface.

Time: Saturday during the waning moon, or on the night of the new moon.

Tools: A personal effect belonging to the target or a small printed picture of them, modeling clay, and a toothpick.

To begin, obtain a personal effect from the target, such as a strand of hair or nail clipping. If you are unable to procure such an effect, use a printed picture of the target (this can easily be done by searching online), making sure it is small enough to fit inside the poppet. Next, using the modeling clay, form the shape of a human body. You may be as anatomically correct as you wish, but even the roughest of renditions will suffice. Use the toothpick to carve out the poppet's eyes, ears, nose, and mouth. Finally, dig a small hole in the stomach of the doll and fill it with the personal effects or a picture of the target. Then replace the clay, filling the hole.

Gaze down at your poppet, and using your powers of visualization, imagine that the doll and your target are magically connected—bound together as one. While focusing upon the doll, recite the following spell thrice:

---

42. Pitcairn, *Ancient Criminal Trials in Scotland*, 612.

Poppet doll, I baptize thee.
(Name of target), you shall be.
Poppet doll, a magic mirror,
To bring my target ever near.
Poppet doll, what happens to thee,
Upon my target so shall be.

From here you might sprinkle the doll with baneful herbs or stick it with pins as a way of causing various afflictions, projecting power through each prick. Whatever you do, you will want to keep the doll in a safe place until the magic has taken effect. When you are satisfied with the results, throw the poppet in the trash.

Part III
Working with
the Otherworld

Equipped with your new tools, along with your understanding of rituals and spellcraft, you continue your journey along the Crooked Path. However, as you round a bend in the trail, you collide with a shrubby hedge that blocks the way. Undeterred, you instinctually step back before taking a running leap over the barrier. Landing on the other side, you are surprised to see a towering tree that had not been there before. Its tall branches seem to reach up into the stars themselves. You then notice the sound of whispering voices all around and turn to see pale spirits moving about the foggy night. Suddenly, you wake to the realization that you've somehow crossed into the Otherworld. Turning back to face the tree, you find a rather benign-looking spirit reaching out toward you. With bravery and intent, you accept their hand, ready to explore the world beyond.

Chapter 7

THE WITCH FATHER
AND WITCH MOTHER

Regardless of whether we consider it a religion or not, there is no denying that Traditional Witchcraft is a spiritual path. Witches are naturally in touch with the Otherworld, and it's one of our primary goals to establish long-lasting, mutually beneficial relationships with many types of spirits. These spirits offer a powerful kinship to those who seek them, and it's through their intercession that so much of magic is made possible. Of the several different types of spirits, many Witches actively work with gods. Although, it is worth acknowledging again that not all Witches align themselves with deities. For those who do, however, there are infinitesimal ways in which the gods are interpreted and experienced. For example, some Witches work with a god, a goddess, or both at the same time. Meanwhile, other Witches work with many different deities all at once. For some, these gods and goddesses are viewed as separate, individual beings, while for others, they may be seen as facets of one overarching higher power. Additionally, some Witches view deities as literal spiritual beings, while others see them symbolically or as an innate part of human psyche. No matter how one interprets deity, it should be pointed out again that in Traditional Witchcraft, these relationships are not based on worship or subjugation but rather equal power and authority.

In this chapter we will meet with the Witch Father and Witch Mother (also sometimes referred to as the Witch King and Witch Queen), the two archetypal deities who are commonly found within the practice of Traditional Witchcraft. As archetypes, the Witch Father and Witch Mother have both taken a variety of faces and forms throughout folklore. Therefore, in order to better understand these two spirits and the role they play along the Crooked Path, we must examine some of their most persistent guises, including rulers of life and death, guardians of the natural landscape, and initiators of the Craft.

The Witch Father

Who is the Witch Father? He is the archetypal divine masculine, the dual-natured god. On one hand, he is the bearer of light, the provider of illumination, inspiration, and life itself. On the other hand, he is the chthonic Lord of the Mound, the sacrificial king who walks among the shadows, the bringer of death. The Witch Father wears many faces and goes by many names; he is not easily pigeonholed into one guise and shifts between them with relative ease. The title *Witch Father* acts as placeholder for the names of the countless spirits which make up his identity. Yet, while he is known by many titles, to the Witches of folklore there was one in particular that summed up this complex spirit. It's a name that causes a visceral reaction, both positive and negative, for many modern-day Witches. For some it is a recoil, as if jumping back from a snake or poisonous plant. For others it is an alluring pull, a deep fascination with something considered dangerous and taboo. Who is this spirit? He's none other than the Devil himself.

Today, many Witches adamantly reject the idea of the Devil having anything to do with the Craft. They will insist that he is nothing more than a Christian construct, a boogeyman who has no place within the practice of Witchcraft. But the Devil of folklore is not akin to the Christian concept of Satan, at least not quite. Without a doubt, this is an extremely controversial topic and one that is deeply ensconced in preconceived notions. It's certainly true that many Witches do not work with the Devil, but this is not true for all practitioners. As we've hopefully come to understand, there are no absolutes in the world of Witchcraft. It's doubtful that there was ever a unified "God of the Witches," just as today we all work with and experience the divine in different ways (including not at all). However, until its modern revival, the Devil seems to have been an intrinsic part of the Craft. Looking back through historical and folkloric accounts of Witches, you aren't likely to find stories of them working with deities like Pan, Cernunnos, Herne, or any of the other popular horned gods of today's Paganism. Instead, you will find them feasting, dancing, and partnering with the Devil.

Be that as it may, many people have postulated that the names of Pagan gods would have been omitted in the trial transcripts by persecutors and replaced with the term *Devil*. This very well may have been the case, considering that any gods or spirits who fell outside of the Christian pantheon were wont to be labeled as devils. While this thought process has undoubtedly caused irreparable harm, with countless people being hunted, tortured, and killed on its basis, it also seems to have had an effect unforeseen by persecutors. By labeling the different gods and spirits as the Devil, it created a catchall that coalesced their unique essences in a workable archetype that survived in the popular folklore. Author Gemma Gary captures this idea beautifully when she writes, "Ironically, it may perhaps be the Church, in its keenness to eradicate adherence to pagan divinity by grafting and projecting it onto the diabolical, that has, unwittingly, most thoroughly preserved the potency, liberation and illumination of the 'Old One' and handed him back to the Witches as the 'Devil.'"[43]

The Witch Father as the Devil is representative of our primal human desires and the deeper, darker recesses of our psyches. When you look at the so-called evils that he is said to embody, they include acts of pleasure, such as singing, dancing, feasting, and sexual intercourse. He is the Man in Black who leads the Witches in their uproarious revelry at the Sabbath meeting. Likewise, he encourages freethinking, knowledge, empowerment, liberation, and rebellion. Remarkably, these are all traits that most Witches would identify with. Of course, these are also traits that the Church has historically been staunchly opposed to in their teachings. Therefore, in this sense, the Devil truly was their enemy, as he stood in direct opposition to their ideology, which has demanded the repression of one's basic human nature. He brings wisdom and insight to the people, although it often comes in the form of mysteries, riddles, and paradoxes. Partly for this reason, the enlightenment he grants is referred to as the *light betwixt the horns*.

As the light-bearer, the Witch Father is connected to Lucifer, whose name literally means "light bringing." Being a fallen angel, Lucifer descended to earth and granted humans with a spark of divine illumination. Within the Italian legend of Aradia, Lucifer is the sun god and brother to the moon goddess Diana. Through their union, Aradia is born and eventually sent to earth in order to teach the art of Witchcraft to those in need of empowerment. As an initiator into the ways of Witchcraft, another face the Witch Father takes is that of Azazel, who was one of the chief Watchers from the ancient Jewish religious text known as the Book

43. Gemma Gary, *The Devil's Dozen* (London: Troy Books, 2015), 11.

of Enoch. The Watchers were a group of angels who had been tasked to watch over humanity. However, they soon began to lust after the mortal women and eventually procreated with them, creating the mythic race of giants known as the Nephilim. During this time, the Watchers also taught humans a menagerie of different skills, including the use of sorcery, herbs, astrology, and how to interpret the signs of the earth.

Besides being an emissary of knowledge, empowerment, and our human desires, the Witch Father is the wild and untamed natural landscape. His presence is felt in the boundless forests and the overgrown fields, during rumbling thunderstorms and windy nights. He is vast, chaotic, and primordial. As nature, he is neither innately good nor evil. Instead he is amoral, capable of both kindness and cruelty. In this role he is the Lord of the Wildwood, master of all beasts. He can be seen in the form of the verdant Green Man, whose foliate face adorns old churches. Recalling the folkloric Devil, his name is given to numerous geographical landmarks— which were believed to have been created by his own hand—across Europe and the United States, from the Devil's Dyke in Sussex to the Devil's Punch Bowl in Oregon. Further links to the land can be seen in the old tradition of leaving small plots of earth—known as the Devil's Plantation—to grow untouched by humans or livestock.[44] Such plots were given as offerings, with a portion of one's property sacrificed to the Old One. As nature personified, he is related to the faeries whom he serves as king and consort to the Queen of Elfame.

But just as the trees, flowers, and herbs grow abundantly in the summer and spring, they soon wither, decay, and die in the autumn and winter. The Witch Father likewise goes through such a seasonal transition, from the Ruler of the Forest in the warmer months to the Lord of Mound in the colder half of the year. Here he becomes the god of death, whose home is within the ancient burial mounds. As a psychopomp, gathering up the souls of the dead, he takes to the sky as the fearsome leader of the Wild Hunt. His eldritch company composed of faeries and ghosts takes to hunting for new members on tempestuous winter nights. Beware, though, for it's believed that to see the Wild Hunt with one's own eyes is surely an omen of death. In a different form, the Devil fulfills similar duties as the big black dog—popularly known as Black Shuck in East Anglia—who

---

44. Nigel Pearson, *The Devil's Plantation* (London: Troy Books, 2015), 11.

prowls churchyards and old trackways. He herds the dead, foretells doom, and occasionally brings death itself to those who meet him. While the Witch Father may be frightening or foreboding during these times, he is nonetheless a powerful teacher. As such, he inducts Witches into the mysteries of death and resurrection, how to journey to the Otherworld and return to the land of the living, unscathed and with newfound wisdom.

FROM THE SPIRITS OF LORE: The Black Woodsman

From the spirits of lore, there is an American story that illuminates the Witch Father's role as a trickster. As it goes, there once was a man named Tom who was walking through a stretch of dense woodland, having decided to take a shortcut on his way home from work. Eventually, he found himself hopelessly lost among the overgrown trees. He had sat down upon a log to rest for only a moment when a tall, dark man suddenly appeared before him. The man had black hair, a face covered in soot, and carried an ax over his shoulder. Tom asked the man for his name, and the man replied that he had been known by many names, including Old Scratch and the Black Woodsman. The mysterious man proceeded to offer Tom the location of a nearby buried treasure. However, it was stipulated that in return Tom must share half of any profits made using the treasure and that upon his death he must go with the Black Woodsman. Being a greedy man, Tom was quick to agree.

With the treasure, Tom opened up a broker's office where he would lend people money at high interest rates with the duplicitous intention of causing bankruptcy. As such, the people were unable to pay back the money and were foreclosed upon—making Tom increasingly wealthier. As the years passed, though, Tom began to worry about his deal with the Black Woodsman. He desired a way out of the agreement and thus began to attend a church in an attempt to appear more pious. However, his attempts were in vain as one day he became furious at a man who could not repay his loan. In his anger, Tom proclaimed that the Devil may take his soul if he had ever made a penny off the poor man. At that very moment there was a loud knock on the door, which blew open to reveal the Black Woodsman. He dragged Tom from the house and placed him on the back of a giant black horse before disappearing. That was the last anyone ever saw of

Tom. That very night his house was burnt to the ground after being struck by lightning and all the money in his bank vault turned to ashes.[45]

The Witch Father can be loving and kind, but he can also be tricky and is not above testing our character. While he isn't likely to take you away on a ghostly horse for your misdeeds, the Witch Father very well might figuratively knock you on your ass. The Woodsman in the story tested the moral character of Tom—and when Tom failed, he had to face the consequences of his actions. The Witch Father can be a trickster, but in such a role he has the power to encourage our personal growth. By turning truths upside down, by testing and tripping us up, the Witch Father pushes us to recognize new perspectives and insights (about ourselves and the world) hidden just on the underside of reality.

The Witch Father is a multi-faceted being whose complexities expand much further than what I have described in this section. There is simply no way to succinctly summarize the entirety of his identity, and it is certainly a task that is beyond the scope of one book alone. How he appears and how he is experienced will always be different for each Witch and decidedly dependent upon their region and culture. There are many possible interpretations and there are truths in each one. Although researching his history and lore is an incredibly helpful place to start, because he is so enigmatic, the best way to learn more about him is to directly experience his presence. I have encountered the Witch Father as a fun and frenzied spirit in the spring and summer, running through the woods with the deer. Conversely, in the autumn and winter he appears to me as a more somber and mysterious spirit, only breaking his silence during stormy nights when his howling voice can be heard on the wind.

EXERCISE 22:
Meeting the Witch Father

Purpose: To meet with the Witch Father.

Location: Outdoors in a lonely stretch of wilderness or indoors in a quiet and comfortable space.

Time: A liminal time of day, such as dawn or dusk.

---

45. Hubert J. Davis, *American Witch Stories* (Middle Village, NY: Jonathan David Publishers, 1990), 151–52.

Tools: Compass-laying tools (pillar candle, a bowl of water, a bowl of dirt, incense, your stang) and an offering of your choosing, such as whiskey or loose tobacco.

Begin by taking a walk to your chosen location (if working indoors, sit down comfortably upon the floor). As you do so, allow yourself to breathe rhythmically and mindfully. Let your thoughts be free to ponder the nature of the Witch Father. Who is he to you? Are there one or two forms of his that you resonate with more so than others? Keep walking until you feel your consciousness beginning to shift. When you feel it's time to stop or you feel otherwise ready to begin, start by laying a compass using the Simple Compass-Laying Ritual on page 61. Then, place the stang in the north and your offering upon the ground in front of it. Take another deep breath and speak the following words or those that come spontaneously from the heart:

> *I call to the Witch Father,*
> *He who is the Devil of the midnight Sabbath,*
> *The master of craft and cunning will,*
> *The Man in Black.*
> *I call to the Horned One,*
> *He who is the ruler of all nature,*
> *The lord of trees and beasts,*
> *He who incites wild misrule.*
> *I call to you, Old One!*

Sit or remain standing, closing your eyes and letting your trance state deepen. Stay in that place until you feel the approach of his presence. Once he arrives, politely introduce yourself to him and then listen to whatever words he may speak. When the time has come for the ritual to end, thank the Witch Father for his attendance. Dismantle the compass by walking the circumference of the space counterclockwise, starting in the north. As you walk, speak your words of gratitude and farewell to each of the directions as well as to the Witch Father and Witch Mother, spirits of the land, and your ancestors. Finish by pulling the stang up from the ground and cleaning your working space. Finally, if you were working outdoors, turn and leave, making sure to return the same way you came and to not look back, as doing so is considered unlucky.

FROM THE BLACK BOOK:
Witch Father Incense

To be used when calling upon the Witch Father.

    1 tablespoon ground frankincense

    1 teaspoon powdered white oak bark

    1 teaspoon chopped pine needles

    1 teaspoon sage

    1 teaspoon vetiver

    5 drops cedarwood oil

The Witch Mother

The Witch Mother is the archetypal divine feminine, in her many different forms. Like the Witch Father, she is principally viewed as being dual-natured. On one side, she is the Cosmic Creatrix, from whom all life emerges. On the other, she is the Weaver of Fate, the old crone who cuts the cord of life and lays out the dead. For this reason, she is at times envisioned as a beautiful, pale-faced woman from the front and a rotting tree trunk from behind. The Witch Mother goes by many names but is also the nameless one, the primordial power, that which is beyond all things. In the canon *Episcopi*—a passage from tenth-century Roman Catholic canon law—it is explained that Witches, under the influence of Satan, ride through the sky with the Pagan goddess Diana.[46] At a later point, the New Testament figure Herodias and the German goddess Holda were added to the mix of women who were said to lead these nocturnal flights. In trial transcripts and popular folklore, she was mentioned as the Queen of the Faeries or Queen of Elfame. She appears in the confessions of Bessie Dunlop, who met her while giving birth.[47] The queen told Bessie that her baby would die but that her husband

---

46. Carlo Ginzburg, *Ecstasies: Deciphering the Witches' Sabbath* (New York: Pantheon Books, 1991), 91.

47. Emma Wilby, *Cunning Folk and Familiar Spirits* (Brighton, UK: Sussex Academic Press, 2013), xiv.

would soon mend of his illness. Later, Bessie's familiar spirit, Tom Reid, informed her that the woman was his mistress, the Queen of Elfame.

As the creator of all life, she is the Magna Mater, or the Great Mother. She is not only the earth beneath our feet and the stars above our heads, but she is also all that exists behind and beyond our world. From her all things are birthed and nurtured, the land, the animals, and us humans. We are all her children, and she walks with us along our journey through life. At the end of our road, it is she who lays out our bodies and prepares us for death. The Witch Mother is Fate itself, the weaver of destiny. In this regard, she is the Moirai, or the three faces of fate of Greek mythology. The triplicity is composed of Clotho, who spins the thread of life and decides when one is born; Lachesis, who measures the thread of life and decides how long one will live; and Atropos, who cuts the thread of life and decides how one will die. In German folklore, Holda (or Frau Holle) is a goddess of birth, death, and rebirth who is said to determine destiny through the use of her spinning wheel.[48] Furthermore, she bathes in a fountain from which babies emerge and possesses a mill that is used to grind the dead into new souls.

Besides creating human life, the Witch Mother is the architect of the natural world, who forms the land and generates the seasons. In the stories about Holda, it is explained that when she shakes her featherbed, it brings snowstorms, and when she does her laundry, the rinse water falls to earth as rain. In Gaelic mythology there is the Cailleach, whose name translates to "old woman" or "hag."[49] There are many variations of her throughout Scotland and Ireland, where she is known as Cailleach Bheur and Cailleach Bhéara, respectively. She is credited with creating mountains, hills, and bodies of water, shaping the landscape with a hammer or mallet. At times, these formations were less than intentional, being the result of stones that had fallen from her apron. Like Holda, the Cailleach has influence over the seasons, especially winter. Legend has it that during the winter months, the Cailleach Bheur keeps the maiden of summer (often identified as Bride) captive in her cave. At Imbolc (a Celtic festival occurring on February 1), the maiden is set free by the Cailleach's son, thus ending winter and ushering in the spring tide. Similar to the modern celebration of Groundhog's Day (which,

48. Judika Illes, *The Element Encyclopedia of Witchcraft* (London: HarperCollins Publishers, 2005), 392–93.

49. Illes, *The Element Encyclopedia of Witchcraft*, 536–38.

incidentally, takes place on February 2), a variation of the Cailleach's story explains that if the weather is sunny on the first day of February, she is out gathering firewood in preparation for a longer winter. Therefore, you always want it to be overcast on this day, as it is a sure sign that the Cailleach has stayed in bed and that winter will soon be over.

The Witch Mother is also the mistress of magic, sorcery, and enchantments. She teaches the art of Witchcraft to all those who wish to learn. In Greece she is known as Hecate, the goddess of the crossroads, daughter of the titans Perses and Asteria. She is a being of liminality, passing between the realm of the living and the dead as she pleases. She is proficient in the ways of necromancy and is an intermediary for the spirits of the dead. Hecate is also skilled in working with plants, particularly those that are poisonous, like aconite and hemlock. It was Hecate who taught magic to Medea, who made frequent use of potions and enchantments. In Scottish folklore the Witch Mother is called Nicnevin, described by historian Sir Walter Scott as a "gigantic and malignant" woman who "rode on the storm, and marshalled the rambling host of wanderers under her grim banner."[50] In Cromek, Cunningham, and Gillespie's *Remains of Nithsdale and Galloway Song* (1810) she is nicknamed the mother of glamour, who presides over the "Hallowmas Rades," thus linking her with the frightful Wild Hunt. She wears a long gray mantle and possesses a magical wand with which she transforms water into rock and sea into solid land. Her magical abilities are similar to those of the Cailleach and interestingly enough, one the proposed etymological origins of Nicnevin's name is *Nc* (translating to "daughter of") and *Nevis*. Ben Nevis (from the Gaelic *Beinn Nibheis*, or mountain of snow) is a mountain in Scotland where the Cailleach is said to live.

◊ FROM THE SPIRITS OF LORE: Baba Yaga and Vasilisa

From the spirits of lore, there is a Slavic story that sheds further light upon the Witch Mother's role as a magical initiator. As it goes, there was once a beautiful young maiden named Vasilisa who, like many other folkloric maidens, was cursed with having a wicked stepmother. One morning, due to her hatred of the girl, the

---

50. Walter Scott, *Letters on Demonology and Witchcraft* (London: John Murray, 1830), 129–30, https://catalog.hathitrust.org/Record/001024364.

stepmother secretly blew out the flames in the hearth and then demanded that Vasilisa go fetch fire from the Baba Yaga. The Baba Yaga was a well-known Witch who dwelt deep within the forest—living in a frightful house made of bones that stood upon a pair of chicken legs. The house was surrounded by fence posts topped with flaming skulls that burnt with an unnerving light. She was infamous for having a capricious temperament and a grotesque appearance—with wild hair and long, razor-sharp teeth. And so, the stepmother felt mighty pleased as Vasilisa dutifully set off, knowing that no one who encountered the Witch would likely live to tell the tale.

Upon reaching the Baba Yaga's house, Vasilisa timidly asked the Witch if she could please have some of her fire. Of course the Baba Yaga was not one to give anything away for free, and so she set about to test the young girl's resolve. The Witch tasked Vasilisa with several impossible tasks, such as sorting poppy seeds from grains of soil. But with the help of an enchanted doll given to her by her birth mother, Vasilisa completed all of her assigned chores. As a reward for her strength and bravery, the Baba Yaga did begrudgingly grant Vasilisa fire. Triumphant in her cause, and feeling transformed from the initiatory experience, Vasilisa confidently walked back through the dark woods with a flaming skull in hand. And when she returned home with that divine fire, the light was so pure and intense that burnt her cruel stepmother to cinders.

In the tale of Baba Yaga and Vasilisa we see a potent example of how the Witch Mother brings about initiation (symbolized by the assigning of seemingly impossible tasks) and gifts enlightenment (symbolized by the fire blazing within a human skull) to those who are successful. Vasilisa was sent out to die but instead returned home, stronger and more powerful, as she had conquered her fears and been gifted magical illumination by the very Witch everyone else feared.

The Witch Mother, like her Witch Father counterpart, is a complex, multifaceted being. She wears many different faces and goes by many different names. She is limitless and omnipresent, existing within us, in the earth and in the heavens, as well as in everything that is beyond our world. Because she is so vast, how she appears naturally fluctuates from person to person. Therefore, like the Witch Father, the best way to learn more about her and to establish the beginning of a relationship is to meet with her directly. In my own experience, I encounter the Witch Mother as Nicnevin or the Queen of Elfame. During the spring and summer months, she roams the forest and dances under the full moon, beckoning me to join her and her host of faeries in their merrymaking. When autumn and winter come, she transforms into the Cailleach, who brings ice and snow. During this time, she demands introspection and dedicated learning, offering her venerable wisdom to those who seek it.

EXERCISE 23:
Meeting the Witch Mother

Purpose: To meet with the Witch Mother.

Location: Outdoors where there is a clear view of the moon, or indoors in a quiet and comfortable space.

Time: The night of a full moon.

Tools: Compass-laying tools (pillar candle, a bowl of water, a bowl of dirt, incense, and your stang) and an offering of your choosing, such as wine or flowers.

Begin by taking a walk to your chosen location (if working indoors, sit down comfortably upon the floor). As you do so, allow yourself to breathe rhythmically and mindfully. Let your thoughts be free to ponder the nature of the Witch Mother. Who is she to you? Are there one or two forms of hers that you resonate with more so than others? Keep walking until you feel your consciousness beginning to shift. When you've arrived or you feel otherwise ready to begin, start by laying a compass using the Simple Compass-Laying Ritual on page 61. Then, place the stang in the north and the offering upon the ground in front of it. Take another deep breath and speak the following words or those that come spontaneously from the heart:

> I call to the Witch Mother,
> She who is the Queen of Elfame,
> The mistress of magic and enchantment,
> The Pale-Faced Goddess.
> I call to the Veiled One,
> She who is the weaver of fate,
> The lady of birth and bones,

She who bestows life and death.
I call to you, Old One!

Remain sitting and close your eyes, allowing yourself to sink further into a meditative state. Stay there until you feel the approach of her presence. Once she arrives, introduce yourself politely and then listen to whatever words she may speak. When the time has come for the ritual to end, thank the Witch Mother for her attendance. Dismantle the compass by walking the circumference of the space counterclockwise, starting in the north. As you walk, speak your words of gratitude and farewell to each of the directions as well as to the Witch Father and Witch Mother, spirits of the land, and your ancestors. Finish by pulling the stang up from the ground and cleaning your working space. Finally, if you were working outdoors, turn and leave, making sure to return the same way you came and to not look back.

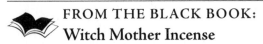 FROM THE BLACK BOOK:
Witch Mother Incense

To be used when calling upon the Witch Mother.

- 1 tablespoon ground copal
- 1 teaspoon lavender flowers
- 1 teaspoon red rose petals
- 1 teaspoon heather flowers
- 1 teaspoon juniper berries
- 5 drops patchouli essential oil

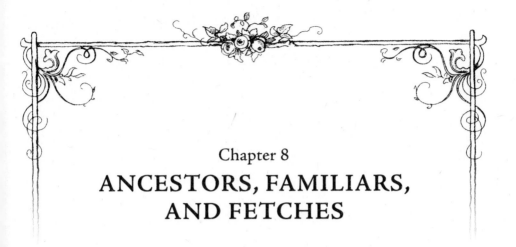

Chapter 8

ANCESTORS, FAMILIARS, AND FETCHES

In addition to the Witch Father and Witch Mother, there are three types of Otherworldly spirits that are commonly worked with in Traditional Witchcraft. These are the ancestral, familiar, and fetch spirits—highly personal and practical spirits who often magically intercede on our behalf. While it's true that the gods are omnipresent, ancestors, familiars, and fetches are typically encountered and engaged with on a daily basis. Some Witches view these spirits as intermediaries to the gods, much like the Catholic saints. Meanwhile, for other Witches, these spirits take the place of working with the gods altogether. In either case, because Traditional Witches work so regularly and directly with ancestors, familiars, and fetches, it is with these spirits that we form some of our most intimate and long-lasting relationships. Meeting your ancestors, finding a familiar, and engaging with your fetch spirit are all important milestones upon the Crooked Path. Having such spiritual beings present in your Craft will serve you well, as they will become some of your greatest and most invaluable teachers, guides, and magical partners.

Ancestors

Veneration of one's ancestors is an incredibly ancient practice, one that can be found in just about every culture and time period. Within Traditional Witchcraft, the ancestors are another grouping of spirits with whom we work. Honoring and giving thanks to our departed kin is important because without them, without their contributions and sacrifices, we simply would not be where we are today. By honoring them, we form relationships that stretch back through time—we link ourselves to a web of memories and to something greater than ourselves. There is a symbiosis to these relationships in that by actively honoring our ancestors, we keep their stories and memories alive. We become the repositories of their wisdom, preserving the collected experiences of the generations before us. In turn, the ancestors are there to guide and protect us, as the continuation of their line—in whatever sense of the word. There is a power in working with our ancestors, one that can bestow upon us a multitude of gifts, whether it's knowledge, healing, protection, or answers to a burning question. They can be some of our most significant allies. But in order to honor and partner with our ancestors, we first need to have some semblance of who they are. While there are many different types of ancestors, in Traditional Witchcraft the primary focus is on familial, land-based, and spiritual ancestors.

Familial Ancestors

Familial ancestors are just that, those spirits who belong to your family. As simple as that may sound, the term *family* is highly subjective and holds different meanings for each person. A family may include your blood relatives, or those people with whom you share DNA. Family can also include individuals to whom you are not biologically related but with whom you still share close intimate bonds. While traditional definitions of family may place greater emphasis on blood relatives, non-biological family members are just as important—if not more so in certain cases. For example, those who are adopted may not know who their biological ancestors are and instead focus on the spirits of their adoptive family. There are also some people who, for a number of reasons, don't have a relationship with their family of origin. Because of this subjectivity, it can be quite helpful to consider your own definition of family when identifying your familial ancestors.

Land-Based Ancestors

Land-based ancestors are the ancestors of place, the spirits of those who have lived and died in the same region where you currently live. This could include people who have lived in your actual house or on the land upon which it is built.

It could also include, on a larger scale, the people who have lived in your city, state, or even country. These are people whose very bones make up the landscape, whose bodies have decomposed and become one with the natural world. Therefore, their spirits are ever present and act as guardians of land, and it's vital that you get to know them by learning the history of your home place. This line of research is apt to bring up important issues, such as the long history of colonization and the horrible abuses suffered by many people at the hands of English settlers. When looking into the history of your homeland, it's imperative to acknowledge the groups of people who were the original inhabitants. In what ways can you honor them and help heal the wounds of the past?

Spiritual Ancestors

Spiritual ancestors, also known as the Mighty Dead, are the spirits of those Witches and other magical practitioners who have walked the Crooked Path before us. As Witches, our spiritual ancestors include historical figures from the distant past, like Isobel Gowdie and Bessie Dunlop. It also includes our more modern forebears, like Gerald Gardner, Cecil Williamson, Doreen Valiente, and Robert Cochrane. It is important to acknowledge the spiritual ancestors because their contributions to the world of Witchcraft have undeniably paved the way for our practices. Their actions in life and the wisdom they have preserved and passed on should not be understated or forgotten. Who really knows what the Craft would look like if it hadn't been for the deeds of those past Witches? It most certainly wouldn't look like anything we are doing today. And it is by honoring and working with our spiritual ancestors that we help further not only our own knowledge and power but also the path of Witchcraft itself.

———

It should be stated that you are in no way obligated to include or honor all your ancestors, whatever the type. There are different schools of thought regarding working with those less than beloved ancestors, such as those who have committed horrible acts during their lifetime. On one hand, it's believed that there is a healing benefit to working with these ancestors, that somehow we can heal the hurt that they've caused and repair our relationships with them. On the other hand, it's also been suggested that we steer clear and only focus on the people who have had positive influences on our life. Personally, I don't feel the need to connect with any unpleasant ancestors, but it's up to you to decide for yourself.

Furthermore, another frequently cited concern when working with ancestors is what to do if you didn't know them personally or don't know their identity at all. Admittedly, this can make connecting with these spirits quite difficult. It's much easier to relate to someone you've already known in life or that you at least know something about. However, this just means that you will need to put in extra effort getting to know your ancestors. In many cases, particularly with land-based ancestors and the Mighty Dead, it's unlikely that you'll have known them personally. In this case, researching and finding out what information you can about their lives is extra significant. If you cannot find any background information on your ancestors, you can still honor them in a general sense, and the more you work with them, the more you will get to know them—potentially even learning their names.

 EXERCISE 24:
Ancestors Reflection

Purpose: To learn more about your ancestors by researching their lives.

Location: A quiet space where you can think and write.

Time: Anytime.

Tools: Your journal and a pen.

Begin with your familial ancestors, exploring your family's genealogy. Start by talking to your older relatives and asking them about their parents and grandparents. What were their lives like? Where did they come from? Try following the trail as far back as you can go. If you were adopted, follow the line of your adoptive family.

Additionally, see what you can learn about your land-based ancestors. Check out your local library or go online to search for information on your homeland. What information, if any, can you find about the past owners of the house or plot of land you own? When was your town or city established? Who were some of the original inhabitants? What details can you find out about their lives?

Finally, learn more about our spiritual ancestors, those Mighty Dead who've helped to further the path upon which we walk. Check out books on the history of Witchcraft, both past and more modern, such as those listed in the back of this book. One text that I highly recommend is Christopher Penczak's *Ancestors of the Craft*, which contains biographical essays on dozens of historical figures who have played key roles within the history of Witchcraft.

In the case of all three ancestor types, consider the ways in which your life has either been directly or indirectly affected by the lives of those who have come before you. Write your responses down in your journal.

 ### EXERCISE 25:
Meeting the Ancestors

Purpose: To meet with your ancestors.

Location: Indoors or outdoors.

Time: Midnight on a full moon.

Tools: Compass-laying tools (pillar candle, a bowl of water, a bowl of dirt, incense, and your stang), three votive candles (black or white in color), a bell, a liquid libation, and representations of your ancestors, including pictures, names written on parchment, dirt from their graves or the land you live upon, or a droplet of your own blood (use a sterile single-use diabetic lancet and wash your hands afterward).

Begin by laying a compass using the Simple Compass-Laying Ritual on page 61. Next, light the three votive candles in the name of your familial ancestors, land-based ancestors, and spiritual ancestors. Repeat the following invocation with bell in hand, before ringing it three times:

Thrice I ring the magic bell.
Come forth, my ancestors, from where you dwell.
I ring once for those of familial bond.
Come forth, come forth from the great beyond.
I ring twice for those of the land.
Come forth, come forth and take my hand.

I ring thrice for those of sorcerous power.
Come forth, come forth and speak with me this hour.

Next, sit before the candles and close your eyes. Call out to your ancestors, greet them, and introduce yourself. In response you may be greeted by several ancestral spirits or only one or two. They may naturally introduce themselves to you, but if not, it's okay to politely ask them more about their identity. Are they a familial, land-based, or spiritual ancestor? You may end up speaking with each type of ancestor or only one. In any case, is there anything that they wish to tell you? Listen to what wisdom they have to offer. Continue to converse with their spirits until the midnight hour draws near a close. Then, open your eyes and with glass held aloft, speak:

I toast to thee, my beloved dead.
I honor the lives which you have led.
I tip the cup and praise your name.
Hear now the thanks that I proclaim.

Allow your heart to be filled with a swell of gratitude as you ponder over the lives of your ancestors. Even if you didn't know them personally, understand that that you wouldn't be where you are today if it wasn't for them. After a few moments, thank the ancestors for communing with you. Give the bell three last rings, then blow out the candles one at a time (you can use these candles again anytime you wish to connect with your ancestors). Dismantle the compass by walking the circumference of the space counterclockwise, starting in the north. As you walk, speak your words of gratitude and farewell to each of the directions as well as to the Witch Father and Witch Mother, spirits of the land, and your ancestors. Finish by pulling the stang up from the ground and cleaning your working space. Allow the libation to sit on your altar overnight before disposing of it in the morning—you can either pour it down the sink drain or outside, allowing the offering to be absorbed by the land.

Familiar Spirits

Familiars are an integral part of the folklore of Witchcraft. Stories of these beings can be found all across the British Isles and in America. There are numerous references to them in the old laws that prohibited Witchcraft and even in the Bible itself. For example, Leviticus 20:6 reads, "And the soul that turneth after such as have familiar spirits, and after wizards, to go a whoring after them, I will even set my face against that soul, and will cut him off from among his people." From these various sources we learn that familiars are given to Witches by the Devil to aid them in their magical workings. William Forbes, a Scottish lawyer in the sixteenth century, wrote that "to some [the Devil] gives certain Spirits or Imps to correspond with, and serve them as their Familiars, known to them by some odd names, to which they answer when called."[51] The spirits or imps were believed to come in the shape of an animal such as a dog, cat, toad, bird, or mouse.

Taken quite literally, the vivid accounts given by suspected Witches about their familiars led persecutors to interpret them as corporeal creatures. It's from this interpretation that we get our modern definition of a familiar as being a Witch's flesh-and-blood pet companion or helper. If you were to ask a practitioner today if they have a familiar, many would be quick to casually point out their cat, dog, or other domesticated animal. There is no doubt that pets are incredibly special and that the bond shared with them is sacred and magical. However, the familiar spirits that are present in classical folklore and the modern practice of Traditional Witchcraft are not physical pets but rather Otherworldly spirits.

There are many theories and interpretations regarding the exact nature and identity of familiar spirits. Throughout time, they have variously been thought to be demons, angels, ghosts, or faeries.[52] It is likely that there is truth in each of these theories and that the term *familiar spirit* acts as an umbrella that encapsulates a variety of Otherworldly beings who act as a Witch's attendant. Regardless, the crucial point is that familiars are *spirits*: they don't take a physical body but instead appear in spectral form. Though, as spirits they do regularly show up in the semblance of an animal such as those noted previously. Other times, they may assume the shape of an animal that is not natural to our world. For instance, Elisabeth Clarke, who was tried in 1645, had a familiar named Vinegar

---

51. William Forbes, *The Institutes of the Law of Scotland* (Edinburgh, UK: John Mosman and Co., 1730), 33, https://books.google.com/books?id=DTdcAAAAQAAJ.

52. Wilby, *Cunning Folk and Familiar Spirits*, 3.

Tom who resembled a greyhound with the head of an ox.[53] Another suspected Witch, Anne Herd, who was tried in 1582, admitted to having six familiars who looked like cows but were the size of rats.[54]

Besides bestial ones, familiar spirits can also take human form, as they did for accused Witches Alice Kyteler and Bessie Dunlop. For Alice, her familiar appeared as a dark man named Robin Artisson to whom she made sacrifices at the crossroads.[55] Dunlop's familiar spirit, Tom Reid, was described as an elderly man with a gray beard and dressed in a gray coat with matching britches.[56] His head was covered with a black bonnet and he carried with him a white wand. It's interesting to note that in these cases, Kyteler's familiar was thought to be a demon while Dunlop's was the ghost of a man who had died in battle twenty-five years before she met him. It's also quite possible for familiar spirits to take multiple forms, shifting back and forth between animal and human as they so choose.

The primary function of a familiar spirit is that of a magical assistant to the Witch. The word *familiar* itself derives from the Latin *familiaris*, which can variously refer to a servant or an intimate acquaintance. At times the relationship between a Witch and their familiar will manifest in the capacity of master and servant, wherein the familiar will unwaveringly perform a Witch's every request. But more often than not, the bond between Witch and familiar is closer to friendship or at least an equal partnership. There is a symbiotic nature at the heart of the relationship, in that the Witch will exchange an offering of some type for the familiar's aid. The most frequently cited offering given to a familiar spirit is that of a Witch's own blood. Bodily fluids, such as blood, contain one's life force or essence, which serves two purposes when offered to a familiar spirit. First, the power embodied within blood provides them with sustenance. Second, by granting them a part of yourself, the psychic bond between Witch and familiar is strengthened. Of course, there are other types of offerings besides blood, including regular food and drink. For example, Anne Herd provided her familiars with a feast of wheat, barley, oats, bread, and cheese with water and beer to

53. Hole, *Witchcraft in England*, 61.

54. Michael Howard, *East Anglian Witches and Wizards* (Richmond Vista, CA: Three Hands Press, 2017), 85.

55. Howard, *East Anglian Witches and Wizards*, 89.

56. Wilby, *Cunning Folk and Familiar Spirits*, ix.

drink. Meanwhile, suspected Witch Margaret Cotton fed her familiars offerings of roasted apples and wine. [57]

What kind of assistance do familiar spirits grant in return for these offerings? There is a long list of possibilities. A familiar may help with spells and rituals, whether they are adding their power to your own or teaching new magical ideas or skills. A folkloric example of a familiar providing a Witch with specific magical instructions is Bessie Dunlop's familiar regularly informing her of which herbs to use for healing when helping cure her sick neighbors. [58] In matters of magic, like Witches themselves, familiars are amoral, ready to help heal or to harm as needed. Jonet Rendall confessed in the fifteenth century that she would pray to her familiar spirit to help heal the sick but wouldn't hesitate to ask him to bring misfortune upon those who refused her alms. [59] Familiars can be called upon for divinatory aid in a variety of capacities, such as looking into the past, foretelling events, and locating lost or stolen goods. John Walsh, a sixteenth-century Cunning Man, would invoke his familiar spirit in order to ask it questions regarding the location of missing property. [60] In a function similar to oracular assistance, familiars can relay information to their Witch about events happening far away. As a facet of this, they can operate as spies, covertly gathering information for their Witch, whether it be to keep informed on a particular matter or to be used against an enemy at a later time. Another way in which familiar spirits can be of service to Witches is by acting as guides into the Otherworld. When we cross the hedge, they can assist on our journey, whether they walk alongside us or we quite literally ride upon their backs like the Witches of old woodcuts, riding astride goats. The Otherworld is their natural home and therefore they have extended knowledge about how things work over the hedge. Familiars keep us safe from becoming lost or otherwise committing an Otherworldly faux pas by showing us the way and teaching us how to engage with the magic of the spirit realm.

---

57. Howard, *East Anglian Witches and Wizards*, 90.

58. Wilby, *Cunning Folk and Familiar Spirits*, xi.

59. G. F. Black and Northcoate W. Thomas, *Examples of Printed Folk-lore Concerning the Orkney & Shetland Islands* (London: David Nutt, 1903), 107–9, https://catalog.hathitrust.org/Record/001648704.

60. Michael Howard, *West Country Witches* (Richmond Vista, CA: Three Hands Press, 2010), 118.

Where do Witches find their familiars? Through the examination of folkloric accounts, it becomes evident that there are three chief methods by which one might obtain a familiar spirit. First off, a Witch can be gifted their familiar by the Witch Father, typically after undergoing an initiatory experience. Mother Lakeland, an Ipswich woman accused of Witchcraft in 1645, confessed that after she had signed the Devil's book, he had given her three familiar spirits (two little dogs and a mole).[61] Joane Wallis, who was tried for Witchcraft a year later, told her persecutors that the Man in Black had sent her two familiars named Grissel and Greedigut who came in the likeness of dogs.[62] The second method of receiving a familiar spirit involves a Witch inheriting it from another individual, such as a family member. Elizabeth Francis, a suspected Witch from Chelmsford, was said to have received a familiar—a white spotted cat named Sathan—from her grandmother.[63] Later in her life, Francis in turn passed Sathan onto another Witch, named Agnes Waterhouse. In fact, according to some legends, a Witch had to first successfully pass on their familiar before they could die in peace. If the familiar spirit could not be given away properly, they reportedly hid in hedgerows waiting for a passing Witch to come along and hopefully adopt them.

Finally, there are those cases in which familiars appear to a Witch out of the blue. Accused Essex woman Joan Prentice claimed that she was simply preparing herself for bed when her familiar, in the shape of a ferret named Bid, first spontaneously showed up.[64] Many times, under these circumstances, familiar spirits would first make themselves known when the Witch was experiencing some form of distress. When Tom Reid came to Bessie Dunlop, she had been weeping over the loss of a cow and for the fact that her husband and child were gravely ill.[65] A Cunning Man in the seventeenth century explained that he met his familiar while walking home from work, feeling heavy with sad thoughts concerning

---

61. Willow Winsham, *Accused: British Witches Throughout History*, (South Yorkshire, UK: Pen & Sword Books, 2016), 59.

62. Emma Wilby, *Cunning Folk and Familiar Spirits*, 61.

63. Hole, *Witchcraft in England*, 63.

64. Barbara Rosen, *Witchcraft in England, 1558–1618* (Amherst, MA: The University of Massachusetts Press, 1991), 186–87.

65. Wilby, *Cunning Folk and Familiar Spirits*, ix.

his family's welfare.[66] Regardless of the specific method for procuring one, it is typically the familiar that finds the Witch and not the other way around. That being said, there are certain ways to be proactive if you wish to find your own familiar spirit.

EXERCISE 26:
Familiar Spirit Reflection

Purpose: Reflecting upon what qualities you'd like in a familiar spirit.

Location: A quiet space where you can think and write.

Time: Anytime.

Tools: Your journal and a pen.

In your journal, respond to the following questions:

+ What type of relationship are you looking for? Would you like a familiar to act as your mentor, partner, servant, etc.?

+ What type of tasks will you be asking your familiar spirit to complete?

+ What type of payment or offering will you give to your familiar in return for their services? Be honest about what you're able to offer and comfortable with offering to a familiar spirit.

+ How long do you want the relationship to last? Some familiar spirits will only be willing to work with a Witch for so long and vice versa. Are you looking for a lifelong relationship or one that only lasts for a certain period of time?

+ How will you communicate or reach out to your familiar when you need or want to? Certain familiars may require a specific ritual or spell to invoke them each time, while others respond just to the call of their name. Are you able or willing to perform such rites or would you prefer something easier?

+ How much communication would you like to have with your familiar spirit? Be aware that some familiars require a lot of attention while others do not. If you don't have a lot of time to devote to a familiar, then you'll want one

---

66. Wilby, *Cunning Folk and Familiar Spirits*, 66.

who is more independent. On the other hand, if you desire a constant companion, then you'll want one who is more consistently present.

EXERCISE 27:
Meeting a Familiar Spirit

Purpose: To find a familiar spirit.

Location: Outdoors.

Time: Midnight on a full moon.

Tools: Compass-laying tools (pillar candle, a bowl of water, a bowl of dirt, incense, and your stang), your cauldron, a paper copy of your answers to the questions in exercise 26, and an offering of your choosing.

Begin by laying a compass using the Simple Compass-Laying Ritual on page 61. Place your cauldron in the center of the space and then sit upon the ground in front of it with your eyes closed. Take a couple of deep breaths and allow yourself to become fully merged with your surroundings. Next, with strong and clear intent, recite the following words:

> *Spirits of the Otherworld, please hear my call to thee.*
> *I seek to find a spirit fine, who my familiar shall be.*

Now, read aloud the answers the questions from the previous exercise. Inform the spirits of the Otherworld of the qualities you seek in a familiar and what requirements you have for a potential relationship. When you've finished reading off the answers, carefully set the paper aflame using your compass-laying candle. Drop the burning paper into the cauldron and repeat the following invocation:

> *I offer up this burning sign in hopes that it shall guide,*
> *A familiar spirit, both loyal and true, to my beckoning side.*

As the paper burns, the rising smoke will carry your call into the Otherworld, where it will eventually be heard by a suitable familiar. When the ritual is complete, dismantle the compass by walking the circumference of the space counterclockwise, starting in the north. As you walk, speak your words of gratitude and farewell to each of the directions as well as to the Witch Father and Witch

Mother, spirits of the land, and your ancestors. Finish by pulling the stang up from the ground and cleaning your working space.

After completing the ritual, you'll need to spend a good amount of time out in nature, dreaming, or journeying into the Otherworld (we will discuss the specifics of hedge-crossing in chapter 9). Keep your senses open, as these are places where you will likely have your first communication with a familiar spirit.

Eventually, when you are approached by a potential familiar, politely introduce yourself and then go over your list again, making sure to ask them what it is that they are looking for as well. If you find that you are compatible, and the partnership is agreed upon, then you can move forward with developing your relationship. If you discover that your needs don't align and that it isn't a good fit, thank them for their time and then keep on looking. Whatever you do, don't settle for anything less than the best. It may take some time, but finding the right familiar spirit is well worth the wait.

The final step in the process involves getting to know one another and starting your work together. One thing to consider is that some familiars may come with pre-established names while others will allow you to give them a name. Names for familiar spirits tend to be odd and whimsical, with historical examples including the likes of Pyewacket, Newes, Elva, Sack and Sugar, Tyffin, Jamara, and Makeshift.[67] Additionally, at times they may have their own personal sigil or seal, which can be used as a tool to summon them or channel their power. The name of your familiar spirit and their sigil (if they have one) are extremely sacred and should be kept a closely guarded secret. In the wrong hands, this knowledge could be damaging to both you and your familiar.

Furthermore, depending upon your familiar spirit's preference, they may wish to be provided with some form of housing. It's important that you give your familiar a comfortable space to inhabit when they're not out and about, especially if they have a mischievous temperament. Possible types of housing include jars, bottles, boxes, birdcages, dollhouses, terrariums, and even animal skulls. Whichever option you choose, furnish it to your familiar spirit's liking. Be sure to include objects that will keep them fascinated and entertained, such as bells, mirrors, beads, and knotted bits of string. Alternatively, you might want to construct

---

67. Valiente, *An ABC of Witchcraft*, 155.

an altar or shrine devoted to your familiar spirit. If this is more suitable for them, consider using specially dedicated candles, bones, or statues, as well as cups and dishes to hold their offerings. On my own altar I have a deer skull that serves as the home for my familiar spirit, along with a candle and a brass bowl that contains offerings.

As with establishing any other type of relationship, it may take some time for the one between you and your familiar to fully develop, so try not to rush the process. The best thing you can do is be patient and maintain your end of the established deal. If part of the agreement you made was that you'd give your familiar a nightly offering or to communicate daily, you had better do so. Failure to keep your word can result in the spirit ending the relationship or even retaliating against you if they so desire. Eventually, the terms of agreement may be changed or revised, but in the beginning it's imperative to be as consistent as possible. Consistency builds trust by showing your familiar that they can rely on you, which prompts them to show you the same level of commitment. If at any point you wish to end the relationship, inform your familiar of your decision, making sure to explain to them why you feel it must be over. In most cases they will be understanding and will part amicably. If not, they can be banished like any other spirit, but hopefully that won't be necessary. Whether starting or ending a relationship, as long as you treat your familiar spirit with kindness and respect, they will treat you the same.

The Fetch Spirit

Within the lore of Traditional Witchcraft, the *fetch spirit* is considered to be a part of the Witch's very own soul. In many spiritual traditions, the soul is believed to be made up of three distinct parts: a higher self, mid-self, and lower self. The fetch is our lower self, which is connected to the Underworld and our deep unconsciousness. As such, the fetch spirit is ruled by our primal instincts. It is the part of ourselves that is motivated by our basic need for things like safety and comfort. The fetch spirit is comparable to the id, the disorganized and impulsive part of our psyche, as described by the infamous psychoanalyst Sigmund Freud. The fetch is also our emotional self, the one who takes in and expresses a wide range of feelings. It is the fetch who, through these emotions, provides us with the power of intuition, those gut feelings which often help keep us safe from harm. By working with the fetch spirit, we can better harness our emotions, attune to our intuition, and access the deepest parts of our unconsciousness. Furthermore, there are special instances when a Witch may ask their fetch to carry out a specific task for them. This allows the practitioner to remain consciously present while another part of themselves is sent out to complete the necessary work.

In appearance, the fetch spirit is often seen as an exact copy of the Witch's physical body. Other times, the fetch—as the ruler of our animal instincts—may assume a bestial form. The morphing between human and animal is, of course, associated with the ancient belief that Witches possess the ability to shapeshift. Folklore is littered with countless stories about Witches turning into animals, especially cats, birds, and hares. Perhaps hidden within these stories are magical truths pertaining to Witches and their fetch spirits, that it is not necessarily the Witch's physical body making the transformation but rather their fetch, whom, in the guise of an animal, they have sent forth to do their bidding. At the same time, though, these folkloric tales also contain a grave warning, cautioning us about the seriousness of sending out the fetch spirit. For it is thought that whatever happens to the fetch, an extension of oneself, will also happen to the Witch it belongs to. For example, a common theme throughout many of these stories is the wounding of the fetch and the Witch later being found with matching wounds upon their body. While it's highly unlikely that anyone would become physically injured from having their fetch spirit wounded, it behooves us to approach this work with utmost care.

FROM THE SPIRITS OF LORE: Peg Wesson and the Silver Button

From the spirits of lore, there is an American story that illustrates the concept of the fetch spirit. As it goes, there once was an irritable old woman named Peg Wesson who lived in Gloucester, Massachusetts, during the sixteenth century. One night, three drunken soldiers decided to pay Old Peg a visit on their way to battle at Louisburg. The men pounded on her door, and when she opened it, they intrusively barged right into her house. Together they began rummaging through Peg's belongings in a foolish attempt to find the Witch's broomstick. Over her angry shouting, the intoxicated vandals continued to harass her until she was finally able to usher them out of her home. As they ran off into the night, laughing at the poor old Witch, she shouted a powerful curse after them, promising that she would take vengeance on them during battle.

In their hubris, the men thought nothing of Peg's curse and proceeded to their destination. But shortly after their arrival, they began to notice several strange occurrences. Canteens would be mysteriously emptied, and they would wake to find that the barrels of their guns had been bent out of shape. Then there was the large crow that seemed to follow the soldiers wherever they went, swooping down in attempts to flush them out of their hiding spots. Eventually, the men realized that the big black bird was none other than Old Peg herself, exacting revenge just as she had promised. And so, they tried to shoot the crow down, but no matter how true their aim, not a single bullet was able to strike the bird. Finally, one of the soldiers, remembering that Witches were said to be weakened by silver, tore a button from his coat and loaded it into his musket. This time, the shot was a success and the crow plummeted to the ground. The men rushed to claim the body, but somehow it had vanished.

When the soldiers returned home from battle, they were shocked to learn that during their absence Peg Wesson had mysteriously died. It was only when the doctor had examined her body that the cause of death was discovered, for embedded in a bloody wound upon her leg were the remains of a small silver button.[68]

 ### EXERCISE 28:
Meeting the Fetch Spirit

Purpose: To meet with your fetch spirit and to ask them for a magical favor.

Location: Indoors or outdoors.

Time: Midnight on a new moon.

Tools: Six tealight candles (white or black in color) and a small mirror.

To begin, prepare the space by arranging the candles in a circle on the ground with the mirror placed in the center. Then, take three deep inhales and exhales, centering yourself in preparation for the work ahead. Light the candles and then stand before the circle, gazing down into the mirror so that you are looking di-

68. Ednah Dow Cheney, *Stories of the Olden Time* (Boston, MA: Lee and Shepard, 1890), 13–18, https://catalog.hathitrust.org/Record/100558500.

rectly into your own eyes. Focus intently upon your reflection and do not break concentration. Allow your thoughts to dissipate and your vision to go soft. Using your eyes, reach down into the mirror, into that deep part of yourself that resides in the Underworld. As you do so, repeat the following spell:

> *I call upon my fetch this night.*
> *Guided be by candle's light.*
> *I call to you, please now appear,*
> *Up from the ground into this mirror.*

Speak words of kindness and encouragement to your fetch spirit until it comes forth to the mirror. If after several minutes have passed you have not established contact, thank your fetch anyway and bid it farewell. If, and when, you do make contact, introduce yourself and begin to converse. The fetch may not use verbal language but instead communicate through a mixture of feelings, gestures, or symbols. It's up to you to learn the language of your lower self. Finally, when the time has come for the ritual to end, thank your fetch, bid it farewell, and then blow out the candles.

The more you get to know your fetch and understand its unique way of communicating, the more likely you will be able to successfully ask it to perform tasks for you. Once you've gained the trust of your fetch spirit, repeat the ritual as described above. This time, though, ask the fetch for its help, explicitly stating what it is you need done, making sure to include the three following stipulations:

+ The task to be performed. Be very specific in order to assure the most desirable outcome and avoid any unwanted consequences.
+ The amount of time granted to complete the task before returning to the Underworld. This is highly important. I wouldn't suggest any period longer than one lunar cycle.
+ The compensation you will give the fetch in return (e.g., offerings of food or drink).

If the fetch agrees, bind the spell by kissing your reflection in the mirror. Then, use the following spell to send forth your fetch spirit:

> *From the mirror, my fetch I send*
> *To do my bidding before time's end.*
> *Go forth, fetch spirit, and make it so,*
> *And then return to your world below.*

Let out a deep exhale, visualizing that your fetch is being released out into the world with your breath. Once you feel that the ritual is complete, blow out the candles. When the fetch has completed its goal, it will simply return to its home in the Underworld.

Offerings

As a sign of gratitude, it's customary to give offerings to your spirits. Our gods, ancestors, familiars, and fetches work hard on our behalf. They have helped open the way for us in the past, and they continue to assist us with spells and magical undertakings. They teach us new lessons that keep us growing toward our full potential and support us throughout life's ups and downs. The relationship between a Witch and their spirits, as mentioned previously, is symbiotic. Therefore, it's our responsibility to make sure that proper thanks are given to those spirits with whom we are connected. Certain spirits prefer to be given specific offerings: for example, the goddess Hecate is said to favor garlic and honey. If you're working with a spirit who has their own recorded lore, look to see if there are any mentions of offerings they are partial to. If you can't find such information, you can always ask the spirit yourself what they'd prefer. There are all kinds of offerings that can be given to spirits, including any of the following types:

Food and Drink: Food offerings can range from a single item to a full-on meal. Baked goods, like bread or cake, are standard options. Fruit such as apples, grapes, or pomegranates are also viable choices. Some spirits may even desire meat or vegetables. For drinks, possibilities include hard liquor, beer, wine, juice, water, milk, coffee, or tea. These offerings can be placed on the altar for a day or two before being tossed in the trash or composted. It might be tempting to leave offerings of food outdoors, but doing so can have harmful effects on animals and the ecosystem. Offerings of drink can be poured outside, so long as they go directly into the ground.

Blood and Bodily Fluids: The classic offering given to spirits by the Witches of folklore is blood. This need not be more than a small drop or two from the tip of your finger. Be safe! Use a sterile single-use diabetic lancet and wash your hands afterward. In my practice, I will dab the droplets onto a small tissue before placing it within an offering bowl. Other bodily fluids may be given as well, but I'll leave the specifics up to your own imagination.

Fire and Air: Fire can be a beautiful way to honor your spirits, whether it's a candle specifically dedicated to them or a blazing bonfire built in their name. Air, in the form of sacred smoke, can be offered by using incense, smoldering herbs, or even cigars.

Water and Earth: Giving water to spirits is a practice that many Witches follow. Water is an ecofriendly offering that is greatly welcomed by the spirits of the land. Earth offerings include sacred herbs and plants that are associated with your spirits. For example, the Witch Mother as I know her is partial to gifts of blue vervain, belladonna, and heather flowers.

Music and Art: Spirits are appreciative of our music and artwork, in whatever medium it may come. Painting, drawing, or sculpting can be wonderful acts of devotion, as can dancing, singing, and playing instruments. The spirits with whom I work often enjoy when I play my ukulele or sing them little songs.

The sky's the limit when it comes to what offerings can be given to spirits, and there are bound to be many more options than those which have been listed here. When in doubt, consider the recorded lore, use your own intuition, and ask the spirits themselves! You're not likely to offend a spirit, but it's a good idea to ask a spirit if there is anything they would rather not be given. Furthermore, it's imperative that the offerings you leave outdoors are environmentally friendly. Even if given with the best of intentions, an offering that is harmful to the earth is a surefire way to ruin a good relationship with the spirits.

FROM THE BLACK BOOK:
Spirit Offering Powder

To be used as an offering to the spirits—left in a bowl upon the altar, tossed into a ritual bonfire, or sprinkled upon the ground.

⅓ cup blood meal

⅓ cup bone meal

⅓ cup tobacco leaf

1 teaspoon wormwood

1 teaspoon mullein

1 teaspoon vervain

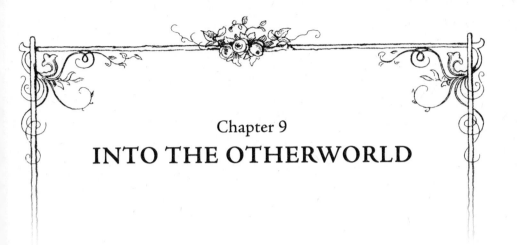

Chapter 9
INTO THE OTHERWORLD

The *Otherworld* refers collectively to those worlds or realms that lie just beyond or outside of our physical one. It's the spirit world, home to the gods, ancestors, faeries, and other assorted eldritch denizens. There are countless interpretations of what the Otherworld looks like, and it has been variously thought to exist slightly above, below, or parallel to our own world. Regardless of specific position, though, the Otherworld is just that...*other*. It's a place that is separated from us by a supernatural boundary, one that is often envisioned as a veil or hedge. Most of the time, and for the majority of people, access to these realms is limited. However, there are places where our world and the Otherworld collide or overlap. These are known as *liminal*, or in-between, places, examples of which include crossroads, riverbanks, and mountains, as well as doorways and windows. There are also liminal times, such as the hours between late night and early morning or the cross-quarter days, which stand as the midpoints between seasons. Witches are unique in that while we will seek out these liminal places and times, we don't necessarily need them in order to experience the Otherworld. Instead, we have the ability to easily pass through the veil and to venture deep into the landscape of that which is beyond.

The Three Worlds

The exact topographical layout of the Otherworld varies by tradition, so naturally each person will have diverse perceptions of what it looks like. The Otherworld is highly fluid and it doesn't operate in a coherently linear fashion, which makes it incredibly difficult to write about in a way that speaks to all experiences. For even on an individual level, one may visit the Otherworld once, only to return later and find that it seems to be completely different from before. Furthermore, like our own world, it's tremendously expansive with unimaginable distances and depths. At times the Otherworld appears similar to our own and at others it is the exact opposite. Up is down and left is right. What's considered taboo in our world is the law over there, and vice versa. All of this may make the Otherworld sound frustratingly confusing, and it certainly can be, but luckily there is some structure to it that we can rely on.

In many spiritual traditions, the world is divided into three parts, an Upperworld, Midworld, and Underworld. Each of these three worlds is inhabited by different beings who call it their home. The Midworld is where we humans live, along with the *Fair Folk*, or faeries. Meanwhile, the Upperworld is inhabited by the gods and the Underworld by the ancestors. This is not to say that these beings are in any way limited to those worlds but that they are more likely to be encountered there. For example, there is an abundance of gods who reside in the Underworld, including the well-known Hades of Greek mythology, the Celtic Manannán mac Lir, and the Norse Hel. Additionally, the three worlds are typically organized in a vertical fashion and are centered along what is known as the *axis mundi*, or cosmic axis. This is the world tree, the central point we experience within the compass round that connects the six roadways—north, south, east, west, above, and below. The Witch is able to travel along this axis in order to enter into the Otherworld, whether that be the Upperworld, Midworld, or Underworld.

The Midworld

The Midworld is both the physical world where humans reside and the hidden spiritual landscape existing alongside it. It's the most solid of the three worlds and is ruled by the laws of physics, science, and logic. The Midworld is associated with the element of earth, our physical bodies, and the psychological concept of the ego. Don't be fooled, though, by its seemingly mundane nature—there is plenty of magic to be found in the Midworld. The earth itself possesses exhaustive virtues and is home to the genius loci, the land wights, and the Fair Folk, who all live within the landscape. Otherworldly journeying can still take place in the Midworld, for in spirit form we can travel to those hidden places within our physical landscape. Magical workings that are typically undertaken in the

Midworld are those that involve physical healing and growth, fertility, abundance, strength, stability, and prosperity.

The Upperworld

While the Midworld is solid, the Upperworld is vaporous. It's the realm of the gods and is related to the element of air, our mental and psychic faculties, and the psychological concept of the superego. The Upperworld can be accessed by traveling up the axis mundi, which is often experienced as climbing the branches of a tree, hiking up a mountain, or ascending a staircase or ladder. When entering the Upperworld, I normally perceive it is a kingdom composed of giant castles in the sky. The magical workings that occur in the Upperworld are those that are focused on mental and psychic matters, including inspiration, communication, enlightenment, and divination.

The Underworld

The Underworld is by far the most fluid of the three worlds. It's the realm of the ancestors and is related to the element of water, our emotions and intuition, and the psychological concept of the id as well as the unconscious. The Underworld is accessed by traveling down the axis mundi, which may involve climbing down the roots of a tree, entering an underground cave, or descending a staircase or ladder. When I journey into the Underworld, I've experienced it variously as a set of underground tunnels, caves, or even underwater grottos. In the Underworld, magic is geared toward emotional factors, including the healing of past trauma, processing grief, and coping with mental illness. Underworld magic also involves working with dreams, intuition, and art.

Otherworldly Activities

There are dozens of reasons why someone might want to visit the Otherworld, but if you were to boil them all down, you would end up with two prime motivations: communicating with spirits and working magic. You will find that in the Otherworld, both of these activities are much easier than they are in the physical realm. Perhaps this is because of the energetic differences, with our world being heavier and denser and thus harder to influence or manipulate. Or it could simply be that speaking with the spirits is clearer in their world and that in turn, they are better able to provide us with magical assistance. In any case, there are numerous Otherworldly activities to participate in, including building relationships with spirits, making pacts, seeking counsel, attaining knowledge, finding healing, and performing rituals or spells.

Building Relationships

We have spent the last two chapters meeting the various types of spirits with whom Traditional Witches work. We know that building relationships with these beings is an integral part of Traditional Witchcraft. While there are many ways we can connect with and honor them in our world, it's also pertinent that we spend time in their world. Just as we cannot expect our friends to come over to our house every time we want to get together, we cannot expect the spirits to always make the journey to our world. Not only does visiting their home demonstrate respect and dedication to the relationship, but by witnessing them in their native setting, we also have the opportunity to gain further insight into who they are and what they do.

Making Pacts

Essentially formal agreements that are made with the spirits, pacts typically involve an exchange wherein we trade one thing for another. For example, a Witch might make a pact with their ancestors in which the spirits provide them with protection and guidance while they give daily offerings in return. Pacts can also be one-sided, like oaths that are made in the presence of the spirits. As such, a Witch may vow to the Witch Father and Witch Mother that they will complete a particular task or abstain from a certain behavior. Pacts can be limited, lasting only for a designated period of time, and they may also be terminated by either party in the case of a breach in the agreement.

Seeking Counsel

There are times in life when we all need someone to talk to, someone to listen to us and occasionally offer feedback or advice. Spirits can be spectacular counselors and, depending upon your relationship with them, can be a great source of support and comfort. Just the same, be aware that many spirits will not hold back from calling one out on any bullshit. At any rate, those who live in the Otherworld have a unique perspective that can help us to find different ways of dealing with those things that challenge us or stand in our way.

Attaining Knowledge

The Otherworld is a place of infinite possibilities and untold wonders. Every time we enter into the realms beyond, we are wont to discover something new. Whether it pertains to spirits, magic, or our own human nature, we return with a piece of knowledge that we didn't have before. You may learn a new skill or a particular spell, or you might discern the truth about a current situation. The information that you learn might come directly from the spirits or from exploring the spectral landscape itself.

Finding Healing

When we are sick, either in mind, body, or spirit, we can find healing in the Otherworld. We can work together with spirits, who possess the ability to deliver curative energy to our bodies, thus relieving us of our ailments. Yet another way in which we can bolster our health is through the Otherworldly landscape, which, like the one in our world, possesses potent virtues that can be used for an array of purposes, including healing sickness and injury.

Performing Spells and Rituals

Any spell or ritual that you'd perform in the physical world can be done in the Otherworld. Any tools or supplies you'd need can be found there as well, but it may take some searching around in order to locate them. Common types of rituals enacted in the Otherworld include rites of initiation, healing, and celebration. Additionally, because the magical energy in the Otherworld flows with more ease and the spirits are more readily available, spells and rituals performed there tend to have a greater effectiveness.

The Witches' Sabbath

There are many things a Witch can do in the Otherworld, and as you become increasingly familiar with its landscape and residents, you'll likely ascertain even more. But for now, let us turn to folklore, where there is one Otherworldly place that has been the frequent center of Witchcraft narratives. It's a place where

Witches gather and engage in many of the activities mentioned in this section. This place, which has been described by a myriad of people both past and present, hovers somewhere between the realms of fantasy and reality, a place that is not quite of this world. As our final stop before moving on to the specifics of how to cross the boundary into other realms, let us take a look at this location, which is infamously known as the *Witches' Sabbath*.

Within Traditional Witchcraft, practitioners regularly make visits to the Otherworld in order to partake in what is known as the Witches' Sabbath. Differing from the modern seasonal celebrations known as *sabbats*, the term *Sabbath* used in Traditional Witchcraft refers to Otherworldly gatherings of Witches and spirits. The concept of the Witches' Sabbath was originally developed during the Middle Ages, as an amalgamation of early Pagan folklore and Ecclesiastical beliefs concerning heresy and demonology. During this time, it was believed that Witches would meet with the Devil at the Sabbath, where they would engage in all manners of magical debauchery. Over the years, stories regarding these Sabbaths gained traction through popular writing and became a central fixture in many of the confessions given by the accused during the Witch Trials. To fully understand the Sabbath's role within the modern practice of Traditional Witchcraft, we must first examine the lore that was generated during the Middle Ages and onward. For it is within the outlandish early accounts that we can find hidden clues to the true spiritual and magical nature of these fantastic nocturnal conclaves.

To attend the Sabbath, the Witches of folklore would take to the darkened skies, riding upon broomsticks, branches, pitchforks, animals, and even on the backs of people whom they had bewitched. Of course, it was commonly noted that these Witches were not physically flying, but rather traveling in spirit form. As accused Lancashire woman Margaret Johnson explained in 1633, whenever Witches desired to be somewhere, they would be transported in spirit upon a rod, dog, or other such item.[69] The meeting itself often took place outside and in liminal settings such as churchyards (between the living and dead), mountaintops (between the land and sky), and fields (between one property and another). In many cases, these settings appeared as Otherworldly parallels to locations in

---

69. Wilkinson, *Lancashire Folklore*, 199.

the Midworld. It was claimed, for instance, that the accused Witches of Salem, Massachusetts, convened for their Sabbath in the Reverend Samuel Parris's pasture.[70] Meanwhile, the Witches of German folklore were said to gather on the Brocken, which is the highest peak of the Harz Mountains.[71]

The specific deeds that were said to take place at the Witches' Sabbath included a mixture of both business and pleasure, with the former typically occurring first. Accused Witch Isobel Gowdie and her coven began each of their Sabbath meetings by recounting their various acts of magic while the Devil recorded them in his Black Book.[72] At this time, the Devil would also instruct Witches on the use of different magical techniques. Moreover, Witches would work new spells and rituals with the assistance of their covenmates. Magic performed at the Sabbath was commonly dedicated to the destruction of enemies, such as when the North Berwick Witches met on the eve of Hallowmas in order to magically destroy King James VI during the sixteenth century.[73] Other official matters taking place at the start of the Sabbath meeting included the making of pacts and rituals of initiation, during which new members were inducted into the coven.

The second half of the Sabbath was celebratory in nature, with Witches participating in a wild rumpus of boisterous music, rowdy dancing, feasting, drinking, and occasional acts of sexual pleasure. It was at the Sabbath that Witches were able to shed the burdens of their mundane lives and partake in those things which were either in short supply, frowned upon, or explicitly forbidden. As mentioned before, the feast would include an abundance of food and drink, which were provided by the Devil or at times brought by the Witches—who had typically stolen the provisions from their neighbors. Music would be played by one or more of the coven members, using instruments such as Jew's harps, fiddles, flutes, drums, and bagpipes.[74] Meanwhile, the other Witches would perform ring dances that were led by the Devil or some other coven official. The coven's revelries would continue

---

70. Le Beau, *The Story of the Salem Witch Trials*, 105.

71. Illes, *The Element Encyclopedia of Witchcraft*, 673–74.

72. Emma Wilby, *The Visions of Isobel Gowdie* (Brighton, UK: Sussex Academic Press, 2013), 48–49.

73. Davidson, *Rowan Tree & Red Thread*, 147–59.

74. Michael Howard, *By Moonlight and Spirit Flight* (Richmond Vista, CA: Three Hands Press, 2013), 32.

until the first light of morning, at which point the Witches would return to their homes and go about their daily lives.

Today, the legacy of the Sabbath continues on within the practice of Traditional Witchcraft, where it is understood as an Otherworldly event, occurring somewhere within the hidden landscape of the Midworld. Here, the Sabbath may be experienced as taking place in a variety of locations, such as on a remote mountaintop or in the middle of a large meadow. To get there, Witches must travel to the Otherworld in spirit form—carried upon broomsticks, stangs, and familiar spirits. Upon arrival at the Sabbath, the scene which unfolds will naturally vary between practitioners, but it is typically one that elicits a great sense of wonderment. What takes place during these phantasmagorical assemblies is quite similar to that which is described in the classical folklore. As a visitor to the Sabbath, you will find yourself dancing in a maddened frenzy, joined by all types of spirits. You will tread the mill to a haunting tune, moving about the compass and performing magic in a state of ethereal ecstasy. You will feast from tables loaded with all manners of decadence and drink from an endless supply of sweet wine. All the while, the Witch Father and Witch Mother sit enthroned, watching over the festivities (and joining in from time to time).

In modern practice, the Sabbath remains a place of immense power where we find the intersection of all three key elements of Traditional Witchcraft. For it is at this Otherworldly convocation that we simultaneously perform acts of magic, communicate with various spirits, and connect with the hidden landscape of the natural world. It is a realm of heightened magical power, and attending the Sabbath is an important undertaking for Traditional Witches, as it allows us to connect with the folkloric heart and soul of Witchcraft. When joining in the timeless eldritch revelry, we are actively living out the folklore of Witchcraft and directly experiencing the atavistic current of our magical heritage. At the Sabbath, Traditional Witches tap into a realm where myths and legends exist as a reality and we play a starring role within them. By embracing and participating in the Sabbath in this deeply personal way, we are also creating new meaning for it within the present and moving into the future. In doing so we synchronically help keep the narrative of Witchcraft alive while also finding our own sense of inspiration, connection, and empowerment.

Hedge-Crossing

Now that we know more about the nature of the Otherworld, let us momentarily forgo our corporeal form and leave the mundane realm behind. Let our spirits slip from our bodies—like snakes from their skin—so that we may walk among the ghostly landscape of the realms beyond. To travel outside of the physical body and visit the Otherworld in spirit form is a practice best known as *hedge-crossing*. Specifically, the act of hedge-crossing refers to a Witch's ability to cross the mystical boundary that separates our physical world from the world of spirits. The hedge itself is a metaphor, referring to the hedgerows that traditionally served as the division between one's property and the untamed wilderness that stood just on the other side. Of course, the unknown depths of nature—with all its wonder and danger—have always been symbolic of the shadowy, enigmatic Otherworld. To venture into that wilderness was to venture into the dangerous territory of feral beasts, dreadful ghosts, and the murky corners of the human mind. Yet, Witches are unafraid of stepping over the hedge and into such seemingly ominous lands, for we already stand with one leg on each side. Further hinting at the Witch's ability to make such spiritual crossings is the Anglo-Saxon word *hæg*, which translates to the word *hedge* as well as to the word *hag*.[75]

But how exactly does one go about crossing the hedge into the Otherworld? Well, like any other skill, it is one that takes time and dedication to learn. But once you begin to practice, crossing will quickly become second nature, with each journey occurring with more ease. To start, you will need to harness the power of your body and mind—through breath and visualization—to alter consciousness and open the way for the spirit to travel forth. Of course, there are also certain tools that can prove helpful, including music, amulets and charms, vehicles for flight, and entheogens such as the infamous Witches' flying ointment. These tools can be of assistance not only in the process of leaving your physical body but also while moving through the Otherworld itself. Although, in order for hedge-crossing to be possible at all, you must have a firm belief in your ability to fly, like the Witches of folklore, free from the earthly limits of your physical form—to transport yourself through the ether and into the spirit world.

---

75. Bosworth-Toller Anglo-Saxon Dictionary, s.v. "hæg," accessed August 1, 2019, http://bosworth .ff.cuni.cz/051483.

Deep Breathing and Visualization for Hedge-Crossing

It's a well-established fact that controlled and focused breathing has the capacity to alter our states of consciousness. Breathing mindfully helps calm the nervous system and relax our bodies, which in turn loosens the spirit. At the same time, visualization can also be incredibly helpful when crossing the hedge. Sometimes the practice of hedge-crossing gets confused with guided meditation or the process of visualization itself. The key difference, though, is that meditation and visualization occur within one's mind, while hedge-crossing can be classified as an out-of-body experience. The use of visualization is helpful for building yourself up to the point at which your spirit departs from your physical body. For example, while engaging in deep breathing, I will often visualize myself actually climbing, jumping, or flying over a boundary such as a hedgerow or fence. I will also envision the axis mundi, or world tree, which can operate as our base for Otherworldly travel.

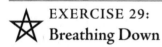 **EXERCISE 29:**
Breathing Down

Purpose: To practice a deep breathing technique useful for altering consciousness in preparation for hedge-crossing, as well as to return to the body after the journey has ended.

Location: A quiet, comfortable space.

Time: Anytime.

Tools: None.

To begin, take a nice, deep inhale lasting about four seconds. Hold this breath for four seconds and then exhale for about four seconds. Hold your breath for another four seconds before starting the cycle again. Repeat this pattern (inhale, hold, exhale, hold) a total of twelve times while counting backward from four to one. Then start the whole process over, but this time complete thirteen repetitions. By the time you've reached the end, you will have reached a deep meditative state in which your spirit will be able to lift from your physical body. When you wish to return, simply repeat the process backward, counting up from one to thirteen and then again from one to twelve. As you do so, feel yourself slowly coming back into your body, wiggling your fingers and toes before finally opening your eyes.

EXERCISE 30:
Axis Mundi Visualization

Purpose: To practice visualizing your personal world tree, which will act as your home base for hedge-crossing journeys.

Location: A quiet, comfortable space.

Time: Anytime.

Tools: None.

Begin by lying down in a comfortable spot, making sure that all distractions are minimal. Close your eyes and follow the steps of the breathing down technique from exercise 29. When you've reached the end of the countdown, envision that a gigantic tree stands before you. What type of tree is it? See its branches stretching high up into the sky, all the way into the Upperworld. Look around the base of the tree until you find an opening in its trunk. This may be a naturally formed hole or even a small door. Look inside and see an intricate set of roots that descend deep into the ground, all the way into the Underworld. Back away from the door and see the whole tree again. Notice that there is a small knife sticking in the ground nearby. Take this knife and nick the tip of your left thumb. Walk up to the tree and place your thumb upon the trunk, allowing a droplet or two of blood to seep into its bark. Feel your spirit connecting with the tree, forming a bond. When you feel ready, back away from the tree and prepare to return to your body by counting upward from one to thirteen and then one to twelve. Feel yourself slowly coming back into your body, wiggling your fingers and toes before finally opening your eyes.

Now whenever you cross the hedge, you will always find yourself starting at the base of the world tree. From there you can either ascend the branches into the Upperworld, descend the roots into the Underworld, or stay on the ground and explore the Midworld. At any point along your journey, should you wish to return to your world tree, simply call it to mind and allow yourself to be pulled back to its location.

Additional Tools for Crossing the Hedge

While you don't necessarily need any tools (excluding breathing and visualization, which are absolutely necessary), they can be very helpful, especially when first learning to cross the hedge. Understand, though, that like the other tools in Witchcraft, they only work as aids and not as substitutes or shortcuts for hard work. They will only be effective if you put your own magical effort behind them. That being said, here some of the most helpful hedge-crossing tools:

Music: Music has long been known for its ability to alter consciousness, and drumming in particular is useful for hedge-crossing. The act of drumming, with its repetitive movement, can be powerfully hypnotic. It is recommended that you make use of a steady beat that specifically mimics a heartbeat and gets progressively slower, which helps lower yourself in a deeper state of consciousness. As your body grows more relaxed, your spirit will gradually be lifted and set free. If you don't have a drum, you can rhythmically tap your open palm over your heart or use pre-recorded music, both of which can be just as effective.

Amulets and Charms: The two main purposes for hedge-crossing amulets and charms are to assist in journeying into the Otherworld and to protect your body and spirit as well. How these devices are created and the way in which they are utilized depends upon your individual preferences. I recommend creating a charm bag that is specifically formulated to fulfill both needs (see exercise 31 on page 136). Additionally, in my practice, I use a special stone that acts like an anchor that helps protect my physical body and keeps my spirit from drifting off too far. During ritual, these items can be placed directly on the body or kept nearby.

Vehicles for Flight: These are tools that can be "ridden" upon in your Otherworldly travels, so to speak, including the iconic broomstick, the stang, and even your familiar spirit. While entering into a trance, lay the broomstick or stang by your side or place it under your knees as if riding it while hedge-crossing. Using it this way will magically help convey your spirit into the Otherworld. Otherwise, you can call upon your familiar spirit and they will carry you upon their back. If none of these options speak to you, consider that Witches have been accused of riding all sorts of things that range from the practical to the absurd, so use your imagination to find something that works for you and your needs.

Entheogens: The term *entheogen* refers to those substances that cause a change in consciousness. In the context of hedge-crossing, these substances aid in lifting the spirit from the body and sending it off into the Otherworld. There are several substances (both natural and unnatural, legal and illegal, and varying in degrees of safety) that have the capability of altering your consciousness. What makes something entheogenic, though, is the sacred, ritualistic manner in which it's used. Within the realm of Witchcraft, one of the most widely used entheogens used in the practice of hedge-crossing is flying ointment.

Flying Ointment

I remember when I first started out on my path reading about flying ointment, a magical salve that granted Witches the power of flight. According to the lore, the ointment was crafted from only the darkest and vilest of ingredients. The books on contemporary Witchcraft at that time assured me that it was only a macabre piece of lore and that it had no use within today's modern age. It's true that when you look into the traditional lore of flying ointment, you'll quickly uncover a dozen or so recipes, each calling for deadly and morally repugnant ingredients. But today, flying ointment has made a surprisingly large comeback within the practice of Traditional Witchcraft. Why? Because when we put aside our fear and disgust, when we sort through the fact and fiction surrounding the Witch's ointment, we find a remarkably strong potion, one that might just do what the stories claimed ... give us the ability to fly.

The concept of flying ointment developed in the Middle Ages, around the same time that the image of the Sabbath was coalescing in popular lore, although the Witch's ointment for flight may have had predecessors going all the way back to the classical period. A popularly cited example comes from Apuleius's *The Golden Ass*, in which the protagonist, Lucius, observes a woman smear herself with a salve before turning into an owl and flying away.[76] An early, and comparatively benign, recipe for flying ointment was recorded by Johannes Hartlieb

---

76. Apuleius, *The Golden Ass*, trans. Robert Graves (New York: Farrar, Straus and Giroux, 2009), 68–70.

in the fifteenth century. He claimed that the ointment was composed of seven herbs, each collected on a specific day of the week: borage on Sunday, honesty on Monday, verbena on Tuesday, spurge on Wednesday, vetch on Thursday, and maidenhair fern on Friday. The seventh component was purposefully left out as Hartlieb feared that people would attempt to make the ointment for themselves. Witches were then said to mix the herbal ingredients in a base of animal fat and bird blood.[77] A century later, Girolamo Cardano outlined an ointment made from the fat of young children, parsley juice, aconite, cinquefoil, nightshade, and soot.[78] Over the centuries, several more ointment recipes would be recorded, each one varying only slightly in its composition. But across these recipes and out of all their listed components, there are four ingredients in particular that have followed us into modernity. They are four members of the same family, each one containing powerful magic and a deadly poison.

The plants in question are mandrake (*Mandragora officinarum*), belladonna (*Atropa belladonna*), henbane (*Hyoscyamus niger*), and datura (*Datura stramonium*). They belong to the Solanaceae family, commonly referred to as the nightshades. Each of these nightshade plants has the ability to produce some manner of psychoactive effect, which is one of the main reasons why they are found in flying ointment. When approached with respect and reverence, they can act as entheogens, helping Witches in their attempts to cross the hedge. However, while these plants' tropane alkaloids can alter consciousness, they can also be fatal when used improperly. We will be discussing plant spirits in more depth in chapter 11, but for now just know that the spirits of the Solanaceae family are not ones to be messed around with. They have a reputation for dealing swift and harsh punishment to those who disrespect them. Therefore, it is absolutely not recommended that any beginner attempt to create their own ointment using these poisonous plants.

Flying ointment appeals to many Witches because it not only assists entry into the Otherworld, but it is also surrounded by a sense of danger that is quite alluring. It's undeniable that there is something about smearing oneself with poisonous plants that have long been associated with Witchcraft that pulls at our

---

77. Thomas Hatsis, *The Witches' Ointment* (Rochester, VT: Park Street Press, 2015), 177.

78. Hatsis, *The Witches' Ointment*, 189.

deep, atavistic longings. But in reality, flying ointment is often a lot sexier in theory than in practice. In fact, there are three major misconceptions about flying ointment that have been widely circulated over time. The first is that the ointment will cause you to have insane hallucinations or otherwise "trip out." This most assuredly not the case, and if you're simply looking for a high, you had best look elsewhere. In my own experience, I've always found flying ointment to be much more subtle, deepening the senses and promoting an overall feeling of lightness in the body. Second, there is the mistaken idea that after applying an ointment, you will be instantaneously whisked away to the Sabbath. Flying ointment is not meant to be a shortcut, and it does not work as an easy way into the Otherworld. Hedge-crossing is still a skill that needs to be learned, regardless of whether you use an ointment or not. Simply applying a salve isn't going to get you into the Otherworld any more than putting a key into a car's ignition is going to get you to your job. Without inputting your own effort, you'll go nowhere. Finally, there is the problematic opinion that in order to be effective, flying ointment must contain poisonous ingredients, especially those that belong to the earliest recorded recipes. But we know better today, due to advanced knowledge of herbalism and medical science. For example, aconite was a commonly cited ingredient, but we now know just how insanely toxic it is and that it should never be used in flying ointment unless you're looking to take a permanent trip to the Otherworld.

The point here is not to dissuade anyone from exploring the possibilities of flying ointment, for when used with the right intentions and precautions, it can undoubtedly be a magnificent tool. Rather, it's to encourage you to be careful and make informed decisions regarding your health and well-being. That said, if you do decide to incorporate flying ointment into your practice, you will be faced with two options, either buying a ready-made ointment or making your own. Each option comes with its own pros and cons. Buying a premade ointment can be an excellent choice for beginners, as you won't necessarily need the same breadth of knowledge you would when making your own. Although, you will still need to know about the ingredients used in its production, their potential side effects, and how much of the ointment to use. The drawback to buying an ointment is that you are placing your trust—and your health—in the hands of someone else. Therefore, it behooves you to purchase from a reputable source. Make sure to check out the creator's credentials and their customer reviews to see if there are any potential red flags. On the other hand, making your own ointment gives you control over what goes into it, including your own magical intention. However, this can be dangerous if you don't have the necessary knowledge of herbs and how they work on the body. Again, for this reason, it is absolutely not recommended that you use poisonous plants in crafting your own ointment. Instead, try using the following recipe for concocting a powerful, non-toxic flying ointment.

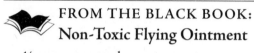 **FROM THE BLACK BOOK:**
Non-Toxic Flying Ointment

¼ cup wormwood

¼ cup mugwort

2 tablespoons vervain

2 tablespoons cinquefoil

2 tablespoons poplar buds

Grapeseed oil

Grated beeswax

Clary sage essential oil

To begin, you will need to create an oil infusion. Combine the wormwood, mugwort, vervain, cinquefoil, and poplar buds in a clean jar with a screw-on lid. Next, fill the jar with enough grapeseed oil to cover the herbs completely. Allow the herbs to steep in the oil for at least three lunar cycles before straining them out with a piece of cheesecloth. You will likely be using only a small portion of this oil infusion. You can store the rest away for later use, although it will start to lose potency after about a year.

The next step is to combine the oil with a beeswax base. You'll want to follow a 1-to-3 ratio, with 1 part beeswax to 3 parts oil. Determine approximately how much ointment you'd like to make in order to find the appropriate amount of beeswax needed. Use a double-boiler system to melt the wax and then pour it into a clean container (such as a small metal tin or glass jar), filling it about ¼ of the way. Then stir in the oil, filling the rest of the container. Mix well and then blend in the clary sage essential oil, adding 10 to 15 drops for every 2 ounces of ointment. Like the oil infusion, the flying ointment will start to lose its potency after about a year's time.

When using the ointment, apply a small amount to the wrists, forehead, and behind the ears approximately 30 minutes before ritual. You'll know it's working when you start to feel zoned out and things around you seem to perceptibly slow down. When you've finished your journey, you can wash off any remaining ointment residue with soap and warm water.

Caution: Be careful when applying herbal ointments to the body as allergic reactions can occur! Always test a small amount on a patch of skin and discontinue use if a reaction occurs. Additionally, do not use this flying ointment if you are pregnant, breastfeeding, or allergic to ragweed, or if you have a heart condition.

Tips on Otherworld Safety

While the Otherworld can certainly be a wondrous place, it can also be quite dangerous. It isn't difficult to stay safe while in the Otherworld as long as you're conscientious and respectful. First and foremost, it's advisable that you do not stray far from the axis mundi on your first couple of journeys into the Otherworld. This will prevent you from becoming lost or ending up in situations that you may not be ready to handle. Therefore, I personally recommend taking it slow, gradually exploring further with each journey, as your ability and comfort level increase. Second, it may be tempting at first to spend a great amount of time exploring the Otherworld. However, doing so can be harmful in that the longer we spend away from our physical bodies, the harder it can be to come back. While it's unlikely that you'd end up stuck on the other side of the hedge, you may start to notice a variety of negative symptoms when you return. For example, you might experience feelings of depression, lethargy, apathy, and dissociation. For this reason, it's advisable that you space out your journeys, limiting them to once or twice per month.

Finally, when it comes to engaging with spirits in the Otherworld, my number one tip is to be polite. Like an interaction with anyone else, being polite is normally the route most conducive for effective communication. That being said, not all spirits are benevolent and it's important that you trust your instincts and enforce your boundaries. This is where protective amulets or a familiar spirit—who can serve as an Otherworldly bodyguard—can come in handy. When first starting, you should try to keep your interactions with spirits brief, and if at any point you feel unsafe, return to your tree immediately.

 ### Exercise 31:
Creating a Charm-Bag for Hedge-Crossing

Purpose: To create a charm-bag to assist in crossing the hedge and protecting the spirit.

Location: A quiet space with a sturdy work surface.

Time: Monday during the waxing moon.

Tools: A pinch of mugwort and one of wormwood (for lifting the spirit), an old key (to unlock the gates to the Otherworld), a feather (to carry your spirit over the hedge), a blue glass bead (for protection from harm), a piece of silver cord (to keep your spirit connected to your physical body), a piece of white or black cloth, and a length of cord for tying.

Begin by individually placing each item on the cloth, informing them of their specific purpose. Next, tie up the cloth with cord before holding it in your hands and charging it with your intention and power. Now, whenever crossing the hedge, make sure to keep this charm near you and it will keep you safe.

 ### Exercise 32:
Hedge-Crossing Ritual

Purpose: To practice crossing the hedge.

Location: A quiet, comfortable place.

Time: Anytime.

Tools: Compass-laying tools (pillar candle, a bowl of water, a bowl of dirt, incense, and your stang).

To begin, lay a compass using the Simple Compass-Laying Ritual on page 61 and call upon your spirit allies. If you work with a familiar spirit, now would be the time to inform them of your intention and to request their aid. Next, situate yourself in a comfortable position within the space. It's vital to make sure that you're comfortable, as any pain or irritation can be quite distracting and pull you back into your body. When you're ready, close your eyes and begin the following process of deep breathing and visualization:

- Start by taking in a couple of nice inhales followed by steady exhales, allowing your breath to come slow and steady, without pressure or force. With each inhale and exhale, slowly count backward from twelve to one.

- Repeat the previous step, but this time count from thirteen to one. With each passing number, feel your spirit lifting while simultaneously feeling your physical body sinking away into the surface upon which you are resting.

- At about number six or seven, envision that you are standing before a hedgerow or other type of boundary, beyond which a swirling gray fog obscures your vision. As you get closer to number one, take a running leap and cross over the boundary. Feel your feet land firmly upon the ground in the Otherworld as you reach the end of the countdown.

- Eventually the fog will lift, and as your vision adjusts, you will find yourself standing in front of your world tree. From here, the journey is entirely up to you, whether you travel to the Upperworld or Underworld or stay within the Midworld. Remember that at any point, if you wish to return to the axis mundi, picture it within your mind and feel yourself pulled back to its base.

When you want to return to your body, take in a nice breath and begin to count upward from one to thirteen. Like before, when you reach number six or seven, envision standing before a hedgerow. Take the same running leap, landing back in the physical realm at the end of your counting. Count upward again from twelve to one and feel yourself in your body, and then wiggle your fingers and toes, before finally opening your eyes. Give yourself a few moments to fully come back into the space. I encourage you to take this time to write down your experiences, as the memory of such events can quickly become foggy. At whatever point you feel ready, dismantle the compass by walking the circumference of the space counterclockwise, starting in the north. As you walk, speak your words of gratitude and farewell to each of the directions as well as to the Witch Father and Witch Mother, spirits of the land, and your ancestors. Finish by pulling the stang up from the ground and cleaning up your working space.

If for whatever reason your first attempt at crossing the hedge is unsuccessful, don't worry. Hedge-crossing takes practice, so simply wait a day or two and then try again!

Part IV
Working with
the Natural Landscape

Emerging over the shrubby hedge, you return to the physical world with newfound insights and spirit allies. Morning has arrived and you find yourself standing in a dense forest with sunlight streaming through the leafy canopy overhead. You can hear birds chirping in the trees, and a few yards ahead a stag runs across the path. You continue walking, stopping once or twice to admire the variously sized pebbles that litter the dirt path and the abundant herbs growing alongside it. The stones and plants seem to be buzzing with magic and you can almost make out their voices calling out to you. Farther ahead the sunlight disappears and a clap of thunder resounds before a steady rain starts pouring down from the sky. You stop in your tracks and allow the heavy droplets to wash over your skin, feeling the power of nature all around you.

Chapter 10
ENGAGING WITH THE LAND

Thus far we have discussed working with magic and working with the Other-world. We've learned about the tools, spells, and rituals commonplace in Traditional Witchcraft. We've mapped out the realms beyond our own, met with a host of spirits, and then crossed the hedge into their world. But now it's time that we focus in on the third and final element of Traditional Witchcraft. For this, we must cross back into the physical world of the everyday and return to our own backyards. We must venture outdoors, into the woods or along the beach, through the desert or up the mountainside, or perhaps just to the nearest park or local green space. We must be ready and willing to get our hands dirty because that last remaining element of Traditional Witchcraft is the relationship that we have with the natural world and the spirits who reside right here alongside us.

Bioregionalism

Within the world of Traditional Witchcraft, the significance of nature and our connection to it is highly emphasized. In fact, we often hear Witchcraft in general being described as a nature-oriented practice, spirituality, religion, and so on. Witches are frequently characterized as being in tune with nature and able to manipulate or wield its power. Ironically, though, it is in our pursuit to establish this connection that we often forget about the importance of bioregionalism. The concept of bioregionalism refers to the significance of things that are local or belong to a specific area of land. A bioregion can be as large as a country but is more often narrowed down to a more centralized location, such as a town or particular plot of land. Bioregionalism encapsulates many natural factors, including the climate, seasons, plants, and animals native to a specific area. It's an important part of Traditional Witchcraft because it is within our local landscape that we can most thoroughly experience the mysteries of the natural world and tap into the immense wisdom and power that lies therein.

However, it would seem that instead of concentrating on the land directly beneath their feet, many Witches tend to follow a system of seasonal celebrations that don't always align with their own region, call upon spirits from faraway lands, and buy herbs and stones that come from distant and unknown locations. Meanwhile, the seasonal changes, spirits, herbs, and stones native to their homelands are vastly overlooked. This is not to suggest that anyone should break up with foreign spirits or toss out their crystal collections but rather to point out the benefit of incorporating the magic that already exists in our own backyards. Simply put, because we come into direct contact with our local landscape on a daily basis, we are much more apt to establish a deep, meaningful bond with nature by attuning to its virtues.

 **Exercise 33:
Creating a Bioregional Profile**

Purpose: To get to know your bioregion by creating a profile of its natural features.

Location: Indoors and outdoors.

Time: Anytime.

Tools: Your journal and a pen.

To begin, do some research about your bioregion by going online, consulting wildlife guides specific to your area, or visiting a local nature center. Then go outside and do some observational investigation. What do you notice in the natural world around you? In your journal, take note of the following:

+ Native herbs, flowers, and trees
+ Native animals (including birds and fish)
+ Nearest natural bodies of water
+ Other natural features, such as forests, mountains, or deserts
+ Nearest parks or other natural areas open to the public

Working Indoors versus Outdoors

Another way in which we often find ourselves disconnected from the natural landscape is the amount of time we spend indoors versus that spent outdoors. While there is a lot to be said about the magic that resides within the hearth and home, it is by directly immersing ourselves in the natural world that we are able to fully experience its power. Of course, not everyone has easy access to natural spaces where they can go to perform spells and rituals. For example, living in a metropolitan city can seriously limit your options of places to go when you desire to connect with the natural world. If you don't live out in the country or have your own backyard, you may need to travel in order to find an area where you can experience nature. Try visiting your nearest park, whether it's a small patch of grass and trees or a multi-acre stretch of wilderness. You might not be able to have an elaborate ritual in these locations, but there are still plenty of ways to meaningfully engage with the land.

In addition to lack of access, there are plenty of other valid reasons for working indoors, including safety and weather. First and foremost, personal safety is crucial and should not be ignored. If a situation is likely to be dangerous, then it's best to avoid it and find a suitable alternative. Refrain from venturing into places where you run the risk of becoming lost or injured. Furthermore, it's advisable to stay indoors during weather such as heavy rainstorms, extreme heat, and freezing temperatures. While it's crucial to face our fears and step outside our comfort zones, especially when it comes to Witchcraft, it's not worth it if your well-being is at risk. Moreover, connecting with nature is likely going to be impossible if you twist your ankle, develop heatstroke, or end up in the belly of a hungry animal.

It's encouraged that you go out and get your hands dirty and your boots muddy. Walk through the woods at night. Stand in the middle of a rain- or snowstorm. Experience the natural world in its rawest form. But it is also recommended that you use your common sense and to make safe choices for yourself.

Genius Loci and the Land Wights

The term *genius loci* (plural *genii locorum*) refers to the spirit of a place. The genii locorum are the guardian spirits of specific areas of natural land, such as mountains, rivers, and forests. They are the collective essence of a location, encompassing all the individual spirits that reside there. When a person enters a natural space, such a forest or cave, the genius loci is commonly experienced as a felt presence, an expansive force that permeates the entire area. Being the spirits of place, the genii locorum are extremely protective, often thought of as tutelary deities in their own right. As such, they watch over the natural landscape with the primary intention of preserving it from harm. Unfortunately, due to the irreparable environmental destruction we have caused, the genii locorum do not take too kindly to humans. At best they are reluctant to be seen, but in those areas where there has been considerable damage, they can prove to be quite hostile. But not to worry, for when approached with reverence and a mutual interest in conservation, the genii locorum can be welcoming and benign.

The *land wights* are the unique spirits that reside in each plant, stone, and animal. Similar to the cells in a body, the land wights are the individual nature spirits that compose the genius loci. In other words, the land wights are the spiritual pieces that collectively coalesce into the overall spirit of the place. However, where the genii locorum are principally concerned with protecting the natural world, the land wights are known to possess an array of different magical virtues that can be of assistance to Witches. Consider that when working with natural items such as herbs and stones, you are directly calling upon the aid of the spirits that reside within them. The land wights carry with them the exhaustive powers and knowledge of nature, both of which they are more than willing to bestow upon those they deem worthy. However, like the genii locorum, they are typically reluctant to reveal themselves to humans. With both types of spirits, it will take time, dedication, and a great deal of respect before they will consider opening their world to you. Remember that they do not owe us anything. We are not entitled to their secrets or magic. This may sound harsh, but it is meant as a reminder that the gifts given to us by nature are sacred and should never be taken for granted.

◊ FROM THE SPIRITS OF LORE:
🕯 The Landvættir

From the spirits of lore, there is a Norse story that highlights the importance of having respect for the genius loci and land wights. As it goes, there were once two men named Ingólfr and Hjörleifr who were traveling to find a new homeland. On the journey, Ingólfr brought with him two special pillars that were intended to stand on either side of his chair at the head of his future household. As their ship neared the shore of what would later become Iceland, he prayed to gods— asking for their guidance in finding an area of land that would be approved of by the landvættir. The landvættir were known to be fiercely protective nature spirits who, depending upon how they were approached, were equally capable of bringing both prosperity and destruction to settlers. For this reason, they were highly revered.

After Ingólfr had finished praying, he threw the pillars overboard, explaining to Hjörleifr that wherever they washed ashore would be the site of his new home. Hjörleifr, though, was less spiritually inclined than his friend and didn't understand the importance of appealing to the landvættir. And so, he irreverently laughed off the other man's concerns, deciding to build his home right where the ship landed. Unfortunately for Hjörleifr, his homestead would never have an opportunity to flourish, as he was soon killed by his servants—whom he had greatly mistreated. Meanwhile, it took three years for Ingólfr and his servants to finally find the pillars. There, they built a homestead that prospered greatly and would centuries later become the modern city of Reykjavík.[79]

From the tale of Ingólfr and Hjörleifr, we can see just how vital it is to have a positive relationship with beings like the genius loci and land wights. Ingólfr was fully aware of the spirits of the land and treated them with due respect. As a result, his settlement flourished. In contrast, Hjörleifr disrespected the landvættir when he arrogantly dismissed their presence. Although it was his abused servants who killed him, I can't help but wonder if the spirits didn't have their own hand in the matter. While his case is quite extreme, this story in particular shows us the different outcomes of engaging with the spirits of the land. When we are kind and conscientious, they can be invaluable allies. But when threatened, they can easily turn on us with a swift vengeance.

Connecting with the Spirits of the Land

Given their hesitant attitude toward humans, you might be wondering how one goes about starting a relationship with the genius loci and land wights. It can take some time before they trust you enough to reveal themselves. The best place

---

79. William R. Short, *Icelanders in the Viking Age: The People of the Sagas* (Jefferson, NC: McFarland & Company Inc., 2010), 14–15.

to start, and truly the most efficacious way to gain their trust, is simply to show how much you care about the environment. Recycle, limit the use of water and electricity, and pick up litter wherever you find it. Further methods include the following:

+ Build an outdoor altar or shrine dedicated to the genius loci and land wights. Construct the altar in a special spot with natural materials. Even if it's only temporary, the sheer act of creating a monument in their honor can be a deeply moving experience. One way you can make this type of altar is by creating a stone cairn. To do so, gather a number of different-size flat stones from the surrounding area and mindfully stack them, starting with the largest ones on the bottom and building upward.

+ Plant a garden that includes native flowers and herbs along with those that attract and support pollinators, which are essential for environmental health. For example, in my garden I always grow meadow sage (*Salvia pratensis*), bee balm (specifically *Monarda media*), and anise hyssop (*Agastache foeniculum*), which are all local and beloved by honeybees, butterflies, and hummingbirds. Your garden can be anything from a large raised bed to a couple of potted herbs on your front stoop. Whatever the size, taking care of a garden allows you to grow your own material for spells and to connect with the land spirits all at once.

+ Buy locally grown foods whenever you can. Not only does this ensure the quality of the food you are eating, but it's also a delicious way of engaging with the natural world. For example, eating fruits and vegetables that are in season is a great way of marking the changing tides. Try cooking and baking seasonal dishes that can be shared with your family and given as offerings to the spirits of the land. Additionally, buying locally is an awesome means of supporting your community and helping the environment by cutting down on industrial farming.

+ Make sure that your offerings are earth friendly! For example, avoid leaving offerings of food outdoors, as they can be harmful to hungry animals. In the case of liquid libations, particularly alcohol, be careful that you do not pour them directly on any plants or their root systems, as this can be damaging to their growth. In fact, one of the best liquid offerings is plain old water, or water mixed with a bit of organic fertilizer. Furthermore, avoid leaving offerings that are not biodegradable.

✦ EXERCISE 34:
Meeting the Genius Loci and Land Wights

Purpose: To meet with the genius loci and land wights.

Location: Outdoors in a wild and private area.

Time: Anytime.

Tools: A bowl of water.

Begin by creating an altar out of natural objects like stones, sticks, and leaves. As you do so, allow your mind to still and your body to become grounded within the landscape. When the task is complete, recite the following invocation before pouring the water around the altar:

> *I call to the genius loci,*
> *To the spirit that fills this place.*
> *I call to the land wights,*
> *To the spirits of the stones and the trees.*
> *Please hear my call and accept my humble offering.*

Sit before the altar and close your eyes. Breathe in slowly and then exhale. Feel the places where your body is in contact with the earth. Imagine that roots are sprouting from those areas and digging into the ground. Allow your energy to meld with that of the land, pulling its virtue up into your body and sending some of your own back in return. At whatever point you feel sufficiently connected, open your eyes. Take in the scenery around you. What can you see? What can you hear? Are there particular smells you notice? Call out once more to the spirits of the land. Introduce yourself and state your desire to meet with them. Then wait patiently for them to come and speak with you. After the ritual comes to an end, thank the genius loci and the land wights for their presence, and then walk away without looking back.

The Fair Folk

A discussion on the spirits of the land would simply not be complete without taking into consideration the Fair Folk. Often associated with the natural world, faeries can be found in just about every culture in the world. They have been known by many different names, including pucks, brownies, piskies, elves, goblins, sprites, and hobs. It has always been considered bad luck to call faeries directly by their name. Instead, polite pseudonyms such as the Little People, Fair Folk, Good Neighbors, and Gentry have been traditionally used in their place. Today, we are most acquainted with the Victorian-era conceptualization of faeries as small, gossamer-winged beings of light. But this representation isn't wholly accurate, and it is most certainly not universal. In fact, when looking into the earlier recorded lore, you will be quick to discover a much different and significantly darker version of these spirits.

In appearance, the Fair Folk are quite diverse. There are those who are diminutive in stature, roughly the size of a small child. Then there are those who are the height of a fully grown adult or even taller. Some faeries are remarkably beautiful, while others are grotesque, with odd physical features. Of course, they are not above shapeshifting and can easily take on different guises as they see fit. The banshee, whose wailing cry foretells of imminent death, is a faerie who alternately appears as a pale-faced woman and a disheveled hag. Furthermore, some faeries may not appear in physical form at all, but instead as a vaporous mist or ball of fiery light. When they do appear in a humanoid shape, they have often been described as wearing human clothing, although commonly in the style of a different time period. Additionally, faerie clothing is usually quite colorful, coming in shades of green, red, and blue.

The exact nature and origin of the Fair Folk has always been a mystery, with different theories emerging over time. One theory postulates that they are actually spirits of the dead who, for one reason or another, have merged with the earthly landscape. It would appear that this belief stems from the existing association between faeries and ancient burial mounds. The mounds themselves have come to be colloquially referred to as faerie hills or forts. Scottish minister and folklorist Robert Kirk described how the Highlanders believed the spirits of their ancestors dwelt within the hills and thus treated them with reverence.[80] Another hypothesis holds that faeries may actually be of a heavenly provenance. According to this theory, faeries are spirits who followed the angel Lucifer when he fell from heaven. In 1871 folklorist Alexander Carmichael recorded a version of this origin story in which so many spirits went with Lucifer that heaven began to empty. In order to prevent further loss, it was ordered that the gates to both heaven and hell be closed. Any spirits who were caught outside were thus barred from reentering and subsequently sent to earth, where they resided within holes in the landscape. The same man who related this story to Carmichael reported that on certain nights the faeries could be heard singing a song:

> Not of the seed of Adam are we,
> And Abraham is not our father,
> But of the seed of the Proud Angel,
> Driven forth from heaven.[81]

The Fair Folk are known to be largely amoral creatures, with the capacity to either help or to harm humans as they see fit. Rarely is a faerie ever completely good or bad, and oftentimes they are simply indifferent toward humans. In the past they were treated with a great deal of both fear and respect, for it was well known that they could be a dangerous lot. While some faeries enjoy playing innocent pranks on humans, others have more malicious intentions. For example, there are the redcaps, who are murderous faeries that are said to pelt rocks at the heads of passing travelers. Their namesake comes from the fact that after injuring or killing a traveler, they like to soak their caps in the blood of their victim. Even the comparatively more benevolent faeries have been known to be short-tempered and easily offended. Take for instance the brownies, household faeries who enjoy doing work around the home while its occupants sleep. Though incredibly helpful when placated with offerings of milk and honey, the brownies quickly retaliate on humans if they feel taken advantage of or otherwise abused. Before attempting any work with the Fair Folk, it's vital that you do your research. Doing so will inform you of what to expect in terms of the behavior of different types of faeries

---

80. McNeill, *The Silver Bough*, 108.

81. Alexander Carmichael, *The Carmina Gadelica*, vol. 2 (Edinburgh, UK: T. and A. Contable, 1900), 327, https://books.google.com/books?id=duMOAAAAQAAJ.

and the proper etiquette for engaging with them. Additionally, folklore will be able to help you determine which types of faeries are best avoided and what you can do to protect yourself from potential harm, such as carrying a piece of iron or rowan berries in your pocket.

Despite their occasional indifferent or disdainful feelings about humans, the Fair Folk have a long history of companionship with Witches. Perhaps this is because of our intimate relationship with the land, which inherently draws us closer to the faeries. Maybe they understand that unlike many mundane humans, Witches generally have more respect for the natural world. It could also have something to do with the allegiance some Witches have to the Devil, who has frequently been known as the King of the Faeries—ruling alongside the Queen of Elfame. Whatever the specific reason, though, these spirits have proven to be of tremendous assistance to Witches and other magical practitioners throughout time. For example, Cunning Man John Walsh told the court in 1566 that he would regularly go to the hills to meet with the Fair Folk, where they would inform him which of his clients had been bewitched and where stolen or lost goods could be found.[82] Meanwhile, Cornish woman Anne Jeffries developed an impressive reputation during the seventeenth century due to the healing powers she had supposedly obtained through her long-standing relationship with the Fair Folk.[83] Like many of the other spirits we have encountered in this book, faeries can provide help with spellwork, divination, and hedge-crossing. And as with those other spirits, in order to obtain their help, we must first develop a working partnership with them. To begin, you will find that several of the recommendations for connecting with the genius loci and land wights will work just as well with the faeries.

 EXERCISE 35:
Creating a Faerie Wand

Purpose: To create a wand to be used when calling upon and working with the Fair Folk.

Location: A workspace with a sturdy surface and proper ventilation.

---

82. Owen Davies, *Popular Magic* (London: Hambledon Continuum, 2003), 70.

83. Howard, *West Country Witches*, 190–91.

Time: Anytime.

Tools: A branch (approximately 12 inches in length), sandpaper, wood stain, paintbrush, wood burner (optional), paint (optional), four strands of ribbon in different bright colors, and small silver bells.

To begin, collect a branch that has naturally fallen from a local tree. Make sure that you ask permission from and leave appropriate offerings for the spirit of that particular tree. If the branch is still fresh, allow it time to dry out before moving on to the next steps:

1. Strip the bark off the branch and sand it down until it's smooth.

2. Apply an even layer of stain.

3. If you wish, use a wood burner or paint to add symbols of personal power to the wand.

4. Take the four lengths of ribbon and tie them at the top of the branch.

5. Along the length of each ribbon, tie small silver bells at even intervals.

EXERCISE 36:
Meeting the Fair Folk

Purpose: To meet with the Fair Folk.

Location: Outdoors, in a wild and private area.

Time: A liminal time of day, such as dawn or dusk.

Tools: Your knife, offerings of fresh cream and honey (preferably local), and your faerie wand.

To begin, walk to your chosen location. Once you've arrived, take your knife and carve a circle (approximately six feet in diameter) in the ground. This will serve as a protective barrier to keep harmful spirits away; remember that not all faeries are benevolent. As you carve your circle, moving clockwise, repeat the following incantation:

> *Only those who are fair and fine*
> *And mean no harm can cross this line.*

Next, set the offerings of cream and honey in the center of the space. Pick up your faerie wand and begin walking the perimeter of the circle, again moving clockwise. Shake the wand in the air so that the bells make a pleasant sound. While circling around, chant the following invocation thrice:

> *I call to the Fair Folk,*
> *To the people of the mound,*
> *To those above and below the ground.*
> *I call to the pixie, the hob, and the sprite,*
> *To reveal yourself into my sight,*
> *So we may speak and dance and sing*
> *Around and about this enchanted ring.*

Return to the center of the circle and take a seat upon the ground. Close your eyes and tune in to your surroundings. Take a couple of deep breaths and be patient. If and when the Fair Folk make themselves known to you, allow the interaction to unfold organically. Whenever you feel that it's time to end the ritual, politely thank the faeries and bid them farewell. Pour the offerings out onto the ground before exiting the circle by cutting a line in the ground. As you walk away from the site, don't look back. At any point, should you feel an unfriendly presence, turn an article of your clothing inside out or put it on backward, which is a surefire way to deter any ill-mannered faerie.

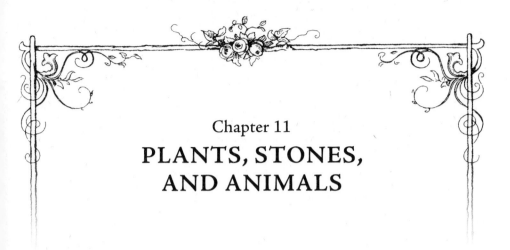

Chapter 11

PLANTS, STONES, AND ANIMALS

Traditional Witches are acutely aware of the plants, stones, and animals that make up our natural landscapes. By our nature, we are innately perceptive and responsive to their magic—from the roadside mullein to the agates hidden along the beach and the mourning dove's song echoing through the trees. Just as we are aided by the powers of the Otherworld, so too are our magical efforts supported by those of the plants, stones, and animals existing in the natural world around us. In our Craft we utilize herbs, flowers, and roots, along with rocks and minerals to enliven our spells with their magical virtues. Furthermore, we discern the hidden messages of animals, channel power through their shed parts (e.g., bones, fur, and feathers), and even occasionally take on their form through the practice of shapeshifting. However, as animists, Traditional Witches recognize the unique spirit inherent in each plant, stone, and animal and know them to be more than just sources of magical virtue. For they are powerful spiritual allies who possess invaluable lessons pertaining to the magic of natural world—lessons they are ready and willing to impart upon those who are genuine in their desire to listen and to learn.

Native Plants

Herbs, flowers, roots, trees, and fungi. Whether it's to cast spells or create potions—both magical and medicinal—these natural materials are immensely useful in the practice of Witchcraft. We blend and burn incenses as offerings to the spirits, we create herbal powders to fill charm-bags or sprinkle over candles for luck, we brew teas and tinctures to heal us when we're sick, and we craft oils and ointments to give us flight. There are endless ways a practitioner can utilize plants in their Craft. Today, we have easy access to thousands of different herbs that can be bought online or in stores. While this access is a wonderful advantage of our modern age, it can unwittingly cause us to forget or overlook the plants that are already growing around us. Returning to the concept of bioregionalism, there is much to be gained from incorporating native plants into our practices.

In comparison to some of the plants commonly associated with Witchcraft, those that can be found naturally growing in our backyards may seem less glamorous. For this reason, many of them are sadly passed off as nothing more than useless weeds. These plants may not have been mentioned in old grimoires or folkloric recipes, but that doesn't mean they aren't magically useful. In fact, they may be even more magical in that they are infused with the virtues of the local land spirits. These are plants that you are inherently more connected with simply due to proximity. You share the same space with them and interact with their spirits on a daily basis, whether you are aware of it or not. Furthermore, you have the ability to interact with local plants in their living state, unlike the dried herbs you might buy at the store or online. You can directly observe how the plant grows and engage with its individual spirit. By doing so, you get to know that plant and how to work with it in a more meaningful way than you would purchasing it dried from a shop.

Start getting to know your local flora by obtaining a local plant guide or going online and searching for native species. Go outside and explore—see what plants you can discover growing near your home, in the park, or even in roadside ditches. If you find yourself being drawn to a particular plant, try to identify it using your guide. However, please make sure that a plant is not harmful before touching it, as some can sting or burn the skin. Furthermore, never ingest a plant that hasn't been sufficiently identified and deemed safe. There are many plants that look similar and while one may be harmless, the other may be lethal. Also, beware of ingesting plants gathered from the roadside, as they may be contaminated from vehicular emissions and runoff. Use your common sense!

Determining the Correspondences of Native Plants

Once you've identified a few of the plants native to your area, the next step is to figure out how you can utilize them in your Craft. In other words, how can this plant help you with what you'd like to accomplish? What magical intentions does it best suit? Customarily, many Witches might turn to a book on herbalism in order to look up a plant's correspondences, or magical virtues. There are hundreds of books out there on the magical properties of plants, but what if you can't find one of your local plants in such a book? Well, in that case you will need to determine the plant's virtues yourself.

There are four main methods that are most effective in determining a plant's magical correspondences, or associated virtues. The first is to investigate any existing folklore regarding the plant, which may inform you on how to use it in your workings. For example, roses have long been said to be sacred to the goddess Aphrodite; therefore, they are commonly used in love spells. To further illustrate, consider how an herb that has been associated with the Underworld in mythology could be used in rituals for contacting the dead. The second way a plant's virtues can be identified is based on its physical appearance and nature. Plants with thorns, for instance, might be associated with the powers of protection due to way those thorns work as a defense mechanism to keep the plant safe from harm. The third way we can establish the magical use of a plant is based on what type of effect it has on the human body. The scent of lavender is very calming, and therefore the plant can be used in spells for peace and healing. Pepper, on the other hand, is irritating to the eyes and sinuses and therefore would make a great ingredient for a hex.

The fourth, and most straightforward, method for determining a plant's magical correspondence is to ask the land wights, specifically the one who dwells within the plant itself. When we approach an herb or root to use in a spell, we aren't simply approaching inert material but rather a living spirit who can aid us in achieving our goals. Therefore, if we truly want to know a plant's magical power, we need to know their spirit first. Conversing with a plant spirit can reveal many things, including that their specific virtues contradict what is contained within their lore. Each plant spirit is truly unique, and that's why learning their virtues directly can be more helpful than looking them up in a book. For example, while a certain text may tell you that mint is useful for encouraging prosperity, perhaps the wild mint that grows along your favorite hiking trail is more concerned with promoting safe travels. Therefore, by getting to know the plant spirits, we not only further develop our connection to the natural world, but we also discover more personal and practical ways of employing herbs in our practice.

During your conversations with a plant spirit, you may come to find that, for whatever reason, they don't wish to work with you. If this is the case, you might wish to ask the spirit for more information about why they feel that way, but ultimately you'll need to find another plant. Remember that not every spirit is going to want to work with you, and that's perfectly okay! There are plenty of spirits in the sea, so to speak.

 ### EXERCISE 37:
Communing with Plant Spirits

Purpose: To practice communicating with the spirit of a plant.

Location: Outdoors.

Time: Anytime.

Tools: A plant.

To begin, consider which plant you'd like to commune with. Once you've chosen a plant, go out and visit it within its natural habitat. Spend time examining the plant's physical appearance and how it grows. Then, either lightly touch or hold your hand directly above the plant. Close your eyes and take a couple of deep breaths, quieting your mind. Allow yourself to tune in to the plant's energetic vibrations the way you would when channeling power. When you feel connected, start by reaching out to the plant spirit and kindly introducing yourself. If the plant spirit responds, you may kindly ask for more information about their powers and if/how they can help you in your Craft. After a few moments, if the plant spirit hasn't responded, thank them anyway and move on to try communicating with another one.

As an example of a few native plants and their uses, consider the following list. However, keep in mind that these are plants that are native to my bioregion and how I personally make use of them in my Craft. Your experiences will vary.

Blue Vervain (Verbena hastata): Similar to its European cousin *Verbena officinalis*, blue vervain carries the virtues of magical cleansing. Druids, Romans, and even the legendary King Solomon were said to have used vervain to cleanse their temples.[84] I recommend using the leaves and flowers of blue vervain during spells and rituals dedicated to cleansing magical tools, the home, or yourself.

Common Yarrow (Achillea millefolium): A staple among Victorian Era divinatory charms, yarrow carries the virtues of love and friendship. As such, it has classically been used to determine a future husband or wife, attract a lover, or make new friends. I recommend using yarrow flowers in spells and rituals for drawing love and friendship into your life.

Broadleaf Plantain (Plantago major): Plantain has been widely revered for its healing virtues. In Scotland it was known as *slan-lus,* or "healing herb." Meanwhile, in America it has long been referred to as snakeweed for its reputed ability to cure venomous bites.[85] I recommend using the leaves of plantain in spells and rituals for healing the mind, body, and soul.

Bull Thistle (Cirsium vulgare): Given thistle's sharp prickles, it is a plant associated with the planet Mars and thus contains the virtues of protection and defense. Bull thistle in particular is highly prickly and makes for a strong magical safeguard. I recommend using bull thistle in spells and rituals for protection and warding off harm (make sure to use a pair of thick gardening gloves while working with this plant!).

Great Mullein (Verbascum thapsus): In the past, it was believed that Witches used the dried stalks of mullein dipped in tallow or oil as torches to illuminate their nocturnal activities. For this reason, mullein plants were often called hags' tapers.[86] As a luminary plant, mullein possesses the virtues of intuition and psychic power. I recommend using mullein in spells and rituals for prophecy, divination, and hedge-crossing.

Red Clover (Trifolium pratense): Clovers, particularly those with four leaves, have long been associated with good fortune. It is generally believed that the four leaves represent faith, hope, luck, and love—although other sources have

84. Paul Huson, *Mastering Herbalism* (New York: Stein and Day Publishers, 1975), 283.

85. Maud Grieve, *A Modern Herbal,* vol. 2 (New York: Dover Publications, 1971), 641.

86. Grieve, *A Modern Herbal,* vol. 2, 564.

explained the leaves represent a balance of the four elements.[87] In either case, I recommend using the leaves (four-leaf or otherwise) and flowers of clover in spells and rituals for luck, prosperity, and abundance.

Harvesting Herbs Ethically and Magically

When planning to incorporate native plant material (e.g., leaves, roots, flowers, etc.) into your Craft, you must also consider how to ethically and magically harvest what you'll need. Right away, it is imperative that you do not harvest plants that are endangered or otherwise legally protected. Doing so demonstrates a blatant disregard for the natural world and will consequently infuriate both the land wights and the genius loci. Additionally, you should always explicitly ask a plant spirit for permission before taking any part of their body. If the spirit denies you permission, accept it and move on. Likewise, a spirit may also dictate a certain amount of their material which you are allowed to take. If you're not given a specific allotted amount, the best rule of thumb is to only take what you'll realistically need or about a quarter of what you see. As always, when you're finished, make sure to provide the spirit with ample offerings in return for their sacrifice. Be mindful when harvesting herbs which may cause potential allergic reactions, burns, or stings!

There are also times, as determined by the phase of the moon and the position of the stars, when plants are best harvested. For instance, it has long been held that the most auspicious time to harvest is between the full and new moon. Harvesting times can be further determined by which zodiac sign the moon is currently passing through. Certain signs of the zodiac are deemed to be fruitful while others are classified as barren.[88] Fruitful signs are those under which plants are best cultivated while the barren signs are better for harvesting. Fruitful signs include Taurus, Cancer, Libra, Scorpio, Capricorn, and Pisces. Barren signs include Aries, Gemini, Leo, Virgo, Sagittarius, and Aquarius. Thus, a waning moon passing through any of the aforementioned barren signs would be a particularly opportune time to harvest plants.

87. Paul Beyerl, *The Master Book of Herbalism* (Blaine, WA: Phoenix Publishing, 1984), 210.
88. Huson, *Mastering Herbalism*, 339–41.

Baneful Plants

Baneful plants are those that are poisonous or otherwise suited for malefic magical workings such as cursing and hexing. These plants, and their use within Witchcraft, are regularly avoided or completely ignored in many modern texts on magical herbalism. While this may decrease instances of foolish people accidently poisoning themselves, Witchcraft isn't always a safe practice, and without a knowledge of the darker uses of plants, we are left with a rather incomplete understanding of herbal magic. This is unfortunate, as baneful plants have just as many lessons to teach as any other plant out there. Though in this case, it's extra crucial that you approach their spirits with caution and respect as they can be harsh and unforgiving to those they find irreverent. But for those they find agreeable, baneful plants can be of tremendous assistance, particularly with malefic spells and rituals.

Before we go on, a word of caution. Handling poisonous plants is dangerous, so always wear gloves and make sure to wash your hands directly after working with them. Furthermore, use separate utensils (e.g., mortar and pestle) for poisonous and non-poisonous plants, properly label stored ingredients, and keep it all out of reach of curious children and animals. Finally, every part of the following plants contain highly toxic chemicals that can cause death. As such, never—under any circumstances—ingest poisonous plants. All that said, let us now take a look at a few ways some of the most common baneful plants can be used in spellcraft and ritual. Please note that these associations are based on folklore and my own personal experiences. Your own relationship with these plants and the virtues that they possess will likely vary. Instead of acting as a definitive guide, allow this list to be a starting point for developing your own correspondences.

Belladonna (Atropa belladonna): The name *belladonna* means "beautiful woman," while *Atropa,* as we know, is the name of the Greek Fate who cuts the cord of life. The belladonna plant itself is both beautiful and deadly. It draws us in with its shiny black berries, which resemble eyes and are extremely toxic. I recommend using belladonna flowers and berries in spells and rituals for bewitching others to get what you want.

Datura (Datura stramonium): In the Victorian language of flowers, datura is symbolic of deceitful charms.[89] This is quite fitting, as datura is closely linked with the Fair Folk and their powers of glamoury and disguise. The large white flowers of the datura plant bloom at night and release a powerful scent, which alone can cause one to feel light-headed. I recommend using datura flowers in spells and rituals for glamoury, as well as for stupefying one's enemies.

Henbane (Hyoscyamus niger): In Greek mythology, it is said that the spirits of the dead wore wreaths of henbane upon their head to help them forget their mortal lives.[90] The hero Hercules is also at times depicted wearing a crown of henbane, signifying his ability to cross into the Underworld and back. The henbane plant, which is biannual, mimics this journey into the Underworld, as it spends most of its first year growing underground before spiking upward in its second year. I recommend using henbane leaves and flowers for necromantic spells and rituals, or those that involve calling upon and communicating with the spirits of the dead.

Mandrake (Mandragora officinarum): Mandrake was once believed to grow at the foot of the gallows where dead men's sperm or urine hit the ground.[91] The mandrake would grow in the earth until being pulled up from the dirt, crying out with a deadly scream. Its humanoid-shaped root grants a sense of tangibility to the mandrake spirit, who has been said to bring wealth, love, and protection to those around it.[92] For malefic magic, because of its physical likeness to the human body, I recommend using the root of a mandrake plant in spells and rituals focused on affecting the body of one's enemy. This could potentially include anything from magically creating mild somatic complaints to actively banishing or binding said enemy.

Aconite (Aconitum napellus): Aconite is said to have been created when saliva from the mouth of Cerberus—the three-headed dog who guards the Under-

---

89. Ernst Lehner and Johanna Lehner, *Folklore and Symbolism of Flowers, Plants and Trees* (Mineola, NY: Dover Publications, 2003), 115.

90. Harold Roth, *The Witching Herb* (Newburyport, MA: Weiser Books, 2017), 199.

91. Harold A. Hansen, *The Witch's Garden* (Santa Cruz, CA: Unity Press, 1978), 35–36.

92. Hansen, *The Witch's Garden*, 36–37.

world—fell upon the earth.[93] The plant was then discovered by the goddess Hecate. At a later point in Greek mythology, Medea (a priestess of Hecate) made use of aconite when she tried to dispatch of Theseus, who was a threat to her power. I recommend using aconite flowers for particularly ferocious protection spells and rituals or workings of exacting vengeance and justice upon one's enemies.

Foxglove (Digitalis purpurea): Sometimes referred to as folksglove, digitalis is another plant that is associated with the Fair Folk. Its flowers, which resemble thimbles or the fingers of a glove, are marked with spots that are thought to have been created whenever a faerie touched the petals.[94] Another story tells us that particularly naughty faeries would give the flowers to foxes, who would put them on their toes in order to silence their steps while hunting. I recommend using foxglove flowers in any malefic working as a means of promoting stealth and covering up one's baneful intentions.

 FROM THE BLACK BOOK:
Hexing Powder

An all-purpose hexing powder that can be used in many ways, including sprinkled over poppets or dusted over the doorstep of one's enemies. Do not consume this powder or burn it as incense!

- 1 tablespoon poppy seeds, for discord
- 1 tablespoon datura, for stupefaction
- 1 tablespoon mullein, for darkness
- 1 tablespoon belladonna berries, for bewitchment
- 1 tablespoon red pepper, for irritation
- 1 tablespoon mandrake, for banishing

Native Stones

Along with plants, many Witches make use of different stones within their practice. The spirits of stones are just as diverse in their personalities and magical virtues as those of plants. Stones are quite literally the bones of the earth; they

---

93. Maud Grieve, *A Modern Herbal*, vol. 1 (New York: Dover Publications, 1971), 9.

94. Grieve, *A Modern Herbal*, vol. 1, 322–23.

are ancient and ever present. As such, they are unbelievable repositories of wisdom and power. The stones most commonly used by modern Witches are of the semi-precious variety, such as amethyst, citrine, and moonstone. Today we have easy access to thousands of different rock specimens that can be purchased, like plants, online or in shops. While there isn't anything inherently wrong with buying stones, there are some drawbacks that need to be addressed.

First and foremost, when we purchase stones, we don't always know where they came from or under what conditions they were sourced. Some sellers will indicate where their stones come from geographically, but just as many leave us wondering where in the world they originated from. Unfortunately, it is sometimes the case that these gemstones are obtained from mines in which environmental and labor laws are frighteningly lax. Second, we don't always know how these stones came to take on their current appearance. Certain gemstones are chemically dyed, treated with heat, or even exposed to radiation in order to enhance their color. Other times, the natural cracks and fissures in gemstones are filled with wax, glass, or other substances to create a smooth surface. Taking these factors into consideration, we can only imagine the upset that these stone spirits must feel.

All the while, the native stones that make up the very land on which we stand get ignored. The stones that are in the mountains, that fill the river banks, or that litter the forests and the fields. Sure, they may not be as colorful and polished as their semi-precious relatives, but they are no less magical. Similar to the plants native to one's own bioregion, these stones may actually be more powerful than store-bought gems because of the innate relationship you already have with them. These are the stones that provide the structural foundation to the very land you live upon, whose spirits are some of your oldest neighbors. Every bioregion will have their own common stones, anywhere from sparkly pieces of natural quartz to smooth river rocks. You won't need to go far in order to find some great local specimens to incorporate into your Craft.

Determining the Correspondences of Native Stones

There are hundreds of books and websites out there dedicated to semi-precious gemstones and their magical virtues. Sadly, there are few to no resources that detail the uses of common, everyday stones that we find while out walking the landscape. So, how do you go about determining the magical correspondence of these native stones? Well, again, I recommend four methods. The first takes into consideration where the stone was found. A stone's location can be a great source of information regarding its potential uses. For example, stones found in the mountains carry lessons from the Upperworld, while those found below ground contain knowledge from the Underworld.

The second method uses the shape of a stone to discover its virtues. Heart-shaped stones, for instance, can aid in matters of love, while flat stones that are rounded and smooth can help with healing. Stones that are pointed or have jagged edges, on the other hand, are favorable for workings of protection, justice, and hexing. Of course, one of the stones most beloved by Witches is one with a naturally occurring hole going through its center. Known variously as holey stones, hagstones, and faerie stones, these rocks have long been used in folk magic for healing, luck, and protection. Furthermore, it's believed that if one looks through the hole, they will be able to catch a glimpse of the Faerie World.

The third method determines the magical correspondence of stones using the symbolism of color. Even the common, non-precious stones come in a variety of colors, and these hues can inform us on how to use them in our spells. Your color associations may vary, but to illustrate the way we can apply them to stones, my own interpretations are as follows:

Red: Protection, courage.

Orange: Success, justice.

Yellow: Knowledge, inspiration.

Green: Prosperity, luck.

Blue: Healing, peace.

Purple: Psychic abilities, spiritual wisdom.

Pink: Love, friendship.

White: Cleansing, blessing.

Black: Banishing, hexing.

Gray: Neutralization, grounding.

Brown: Home, family.

The fourth method, like the one we used for plants, involves directly asking the spirit of the stone about its virtues. To do so, simply follow the same instructions as listed in exercise 37 (see page 156). Again, you may find that, for whatever reason, a stone spirit doesn't wish to help you, and that's perfectly all right. There have been plenty of times when I've picked up a stone that I thought would be useful in a spell only to have the stone ask me to put it right back down. It's important that we respect the desires of the spirits and the boundaries they enforce. As always, make sure to properly thank the stone spirit at the end of your conversation, regardless of whether or not it has chosen to help you.

 EXERCISE 38:
Creating an Enchanted Stone

Purpose: To enchant a stone by painting it with symbols of magical intention, to be kept in special places, used in charm-bags, buried in the ground, or given away.

Location: A quiet place with a sturdy work surface.

Time: Anytime.

Tools: A stone found in your local landscape, paint, and a paintbrush.

To begin, consider your magical intention. Then, go outside and look around until you find a rock that is suitable to your needs. Pay attention to the location, shape, and color. Also, make sure to ask the stone spirit if they would like to assist you with your magical endeavor. If the spirit agrees, thank them and bring the stone home. If not, thank the spirit anyway and then put the stone back where you found it. Once you've collected a stone, determine which symbols (such as pentagrams, runes, astrological signs, etc.) you'll be using to enchant it with. Next, paint your chosen symbols accordingly and then allow time for the stone to dry. Finally, hallow the stone by blowing on it three times and informing it of its magical purpose. You can carry the finished stone in your pocket, add it to a charm-bag, or leave it upon your altar.

Animals

Just as important as the plants and stones that make up our landscape are the wild animals with whom we share it. Animals are innately magical, being far more in tune with the rhythms and tides of the natural world than we are as humans. Consequently, they are also more aware of and connected to the genius loci, land wights, and Fair Folk. In general, there is a sense of otherness to animals that has long captivated and frightened humans. We have always worried about the wild animals deemed dangerous, afraid of being caught in their teeth and claws. Yet, we are captivated and overcome with wonder by their nature, which at times is eerily similar to our own. Call to mind those times when people's behavior and personality are compared to those of animals, such as when a person is referred to as a pig because they are messy or a fox because they are sly. It would appear that the line that separates man from beast is only a thin one at best. And for those people who possess the magical ability to do so, that line can be crossed.

Witches have timelessly been credited with the ability to not only communicate with animals but turn into them as well. In our modern practice, we have the power to speak with the animals of our local landscape and to learn valuable lessons from them about life, death, and the deeper workings of the natural world. These marvelous creatures can assist us in our magical workings with their physical and spiritual presence, as well as through the use of their naturally shed parts, which can be invaluable ingredients for spells and charms. All we need to do is step outside, open our eyes, and become aware of the animals that reside in our bioregion of the world. Get to know the mammals, amphibians, reptiles, birds, fish, and insects that live alongside you and you'll soon come to find the significant role they play within the practice of Traditional Witchcraft.

Augury

Animals are incredibly talkative creatures, whether we are aware of it or not. They have a lot to say about the natural world and are exemplary messengers, providing information regarding both physical and spiritual matters. It is when we start to pay attention, opening our eyes and ears to the animals around us, that we can become privy to these valuable messages. We become able to interpret the signs and omens they convey. This practice of interpreting signs and omens based on the observation of animal behavior is known as *augury*. It's a practice that is remarkably useful but can take some time to learn, as you'll need to collect quite a lot of observational data before patterns and meanings can be determined. But the more we are actively aware of the animals in our bioregion, the easier this data collection process becomes and the more receptive we will be to the messages they are sending to us.

The easiest way to start practicing augury is to select one native animal to observe. It's not uncommon for a Witch to know one or two animals that are particularly vocal. For example, I tend to have a lot of conversations with the crows, geese, deer, and toads around the area where I live. Once you've selected an animal, study up on its appearance, physical abilities, and habits. The virtues and wisdom each animal possesses can typically be found mirrored in these traits. For example, because of their habit of feasting upon carcasses, crows are commonly associated with the spirits of the dead. Therefore, you might view a crow appearing on your windowsill as an indication that one of your ancestral spirits is trying to communicate. In addition, you can find a plethora of information about the inherent virtues of each animal by exploring the folklore associated with them. Another way of interpreting the behavior of an animal is to pay attention to its movements whenever it appears, especially the direction from which it approaches. An animal approaching from the right signifies good fortune, blessings, and things that are increasing or that pertain to the future. Meanwhile, an animal that comes from the left signals a warning, misfortune, and things that are decreasing or deal with the past. Thus, a crow swooping across your path from the left-hand side may be a warning that your current course of action is ill-advised, while one coming from the right might suggest that luck is on your side. Further interpretations can be determined based on numbers, such as how many of a particular animal are in one place at a given time. Generally speaking, the higher the number, the more salient the message. For example, ten crows flying to the left may signify much more substantial misfortune than one or two crows.

As you take note of the animals in your landscape and their behavioral patterns, keep track of these observations in your journal. Write down what you've witnessed as well as what you were doing and feeling in that particular moment. Later on, go back and add any follow-up information regarding particular events that might have stood out during the rest of that day. This will become your database from which patterns and interpretation will emerge over time. For instance, you may look back and discover that the times you've encountered frogs, you were met with a streak of good luck shortly thereafter. Or perhaps a butterfly flying through your window is regularly followed by an unexpected visitor dropping by. Naturally, you'll come to find that certain animals and behaviors hold different meanings for you than those recorded by other people. While one practitioner may view bears as a symbol of strength, you may see them as a sign of danger. While one practitioner may interpret odd numbers of geese to be a negative omen, you may see it as incredibly lucky. Of course, the more you get to know each animal, the more straightforward and consequential these messages will become.

Bones, Fur, and Feathers

One way we might incorporate the local wildlife into our practice is by making use of their naturally shed parts, such as bones, fur, and feathers. It must be emphasized, though, that these parts must be *naturally* shed. Under no circumstances is an animal to be harmed or killed solely to obtain their bones, fur, or feathers. Of course, this does not include hunting that is done legally and ethically, with all parts of the fallen animal being used respectfully. In addition, before collecting parts that you find out in nature, make sure that it is legally and spiritually okay to do so. Check out your local laws, which may regulate if and when certain animal parts can be collected. For example, in North America, the Migratory Bird Treaty Act of 1918 outlaws the collection and possession of migratory bird feathers.[95] Even if it you are allowed to legally take animal parts, you will still need to ask permission from the spirits of the land as well. Finally, if you plan on buying animal parts, be conscientious about the seller's credentials (e.g., if they have permits to be selling these items) and under what conditions they obtained the parts.

All that said, how does one go about using animal parts in their Craft? Through my own experience, I have come to categorize these parts into three loose categories: bones, fur, and feathers. Each of these categories corresponds with the energies of the three worlds, with bones being associated with the Underworld, fur with the Midworld, and feathers with the Upperworld. Thus, these parts contain the virtues of those realms along with those of the animal to which

---

95. For a full list of protected species, visit https://www.fws.gov/birds/management /managed-species/migratory-bird-treaty-act-protected-species.php.

they belonged. As symbols of life and death, bones (including teeth and claws) can be used as tools in rituals for communing with the ancestors, as well as in spells for healing and hexing. Fur, which shields animals from the cold, is useful for connecting to the spirits of the land, as a tool for shapeshifting, and in spells for prosperity and protection. Feathers help our avian friends soar heavenward, and they can do much the same for Witches, carrying our prayers to the gods, aiding in Otherworldly flight and in spells for cleansing and communication.

Shapeshifting

Throughout the folklore of the world, there are stories about humans with the ability to transform themselves into animals. Perhaps the most recognizable of such stories are those pertaining to the werewolf, who has permutations in several different cultures across the globe. The werewolf's transformation is usually described as being uncontrollable, the result of an ancient curse. Witches, on the other hand, have been reputed to be able to metamorphose whenever they so choose and into a variety of animal forms. Ann Armstrong, an accused Witch from 1673 Northumberland, reported that one of her covenmates had transformed herself into four different animals during one Sabbath meeting. According to Armstrong, the other Witch had shapeshifted into a cat, hare, greyhound, and bee, all to prove her power to the Devil.[96] Isobel Gowdie not only confessed to having transformed into a hare, cat, and crow, but she also provided the spells, shown in the three excerpts below, which were used to make such transformations:

> I sall goe intill ane haire,
> With sorrow, and sych, and meikle caire;
> And I sall goe in the Divellis nam,
> Ay whill I com hom [againe!]

> I sall goe [in til ane catt,]
> [With sorrow, and sych, and a blak] shot!
> And I sall goe in the Divellis nam,
> Ay quhill I com hom again!

> I sall goe intill a craw,
> With sorrow, and sych, and a blak [thraw!

---

96. Hole, *Witchcraft in England*, 125.

And I sall goe in the Divellis name,]
Ay quhill I com hom again![97]

In actual practice, shapeshifting does not happen in the physical sense but rather in a spiritual context. It is the Witch's spirit that undergoes the animal trans-formation while traveling about the Otherworld. To achieve such a feat, the Witch must concentrate their power on morphing the spirit body into animal form. As spirits, our bodies are vaporous and highly malleable, making it relatively easy for shapeshifting to occur. However, through this process, we take on not only the ap-pearance of an animal but their skills and magical virtues as well. Thus, shapeshift-ing is an advantageous practice for Witches in that it allows us to channel the wisdom and power of animals. Furthermore, we can learn more about the natural world by experiencing it from an animal perspective—giving a whole new meaning to the sentiment of seeing the world through someone else's eyes.

 EXERCISE 39:
Shapeshifting Ritual

Purpose: To practice shapeshifting into animal form.

Location: A quiet, comfortable space.

Time: Anytime.

Tools: Compass-laying tools (pillar candle, a bowl of water, a bowl of dirt, in-cense, and your stang) and a representational item of the animal whose form you'll be taking, such as a naturally shed part, a picture, or a small carving.

To begin, you will need to choose an animal whose shape you'd like to take. I recommend that you pick an animal that is common to your bioregion and who you're familiar with in terms of their anatomy and physical abilities. Once you've decided upon an animal, proceed to lay a compass using the Simple Compass-Laying Ritual on page 61. Next, lie down on the floor, making sure to position yourself comfortably, either holding your representational item or hav-ing it close to your body. When you're ready, perform the hedge-crossing ritual as described in exercise 32 (see page 136). Once you've arrived in the Otherworld,

---

97. Pitcairn, *Ancient Criminal Trials in Scotland*, 607–8. Brackets are Pitcairn's.

start your transformation by focusing on your chosen animal and repeating the following Gowdie-inspired spell thrice:

> *As a (name of animal) I shall go,*
> *Up above and down below,*
> *And in this shape I shall roam,*
> *Until I wish to come back home.*

Now, focus on your spirit body stretching, shrinking, and otherwise contorting into that of your chosen animal. After the transformation is complete, you are free to traverse the realms in your new animal form. Whenever you wish to transform back, simply say, *I wish to come home,* and focus on your animal body reverting back into your human one.

When you're ready to return to the physical world, take in a nice breath and proceed to count upward from one to thirteen. When you reach number six or seven, envision standing before a hedgerow. Take a running leap over the hedge, landing back in the mundane realm at the end of your counting. Count upward again from twelve to one and feel yourself in your body, wiggle your fingers and toes, before finally opening your eyes. Give yourself a few moments to fully come back into the space.

Finally, dismantle the compass by walking the circumference of the space counterclockwise, starting in the north. As you walk, speak your words of gratitude and farewell to each of the directions as well as to the Witch Father and Witch Mother, spirits of the land, and your ancestors. Finish by pulling the stang up from the ground and cleaning your working space.

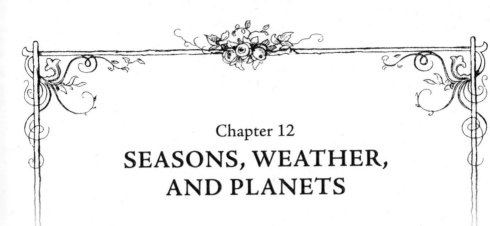

Chapter 12
SEASONS, WEATHER, AND PLANETS

Beyond the plants, stones, and animals of our bioregions, Traditional Witches also regularly work with the cycles of the seasons, weather patterns, and planetary influences. Whether it's the first day of spring, a lightning storm, or the night of a new moon, Witches know that there are certain times when the conditions for magic are just right. For within the shifting seasonal, meteorological, and astronomical movements, there is power. But being more than mere sources of external magic, they are also mirrors through which our own internal processes are reflected. We are all subject to our own physical, mental, emotional, and spiritual cycles—which are often in alignment with the seasons, weather, and planets. However, as Witches, we have the ability to harness the power of these cycles—both internal and external—in order to further unlock the mysteries and magic of the landscape around us, to learn more about the workings of the natural world and how to wield its magnificent power.

Seasonal Tides

Having a profound effect upon humans, animals, and spirits alike, the shifting seasonal tides bring a host of physical, mental, emotional, and spiritual changes. Unlike many modern folk, Witches have remained acutely aware of these seasonal changes and the energetic ebb and flow that accompany them. Hence, we are able to tap into these natural rhythms and channel their power to deepen our connection with the land and to manifest our magical intentions. But in order to do so, we must first become cognizant of how each season alters not only the natural world but us as well. While the energy of each season is relatively consistent, how they physically manifest varies by each bioregion. Therefore, you may need to adjust the following material according to your own landscape.

Autumn Tide

With the coming of autumn, the sun begins to decline in strength and the natural world prepares itself for a long sleep. We can see this in the plants, which shed their foliage and turn their attention to preserving and fortifying their root systems. The trees drop their leaves and start the process of going dormant, which keeps them alive throughout the colder months. Animals work to store food or pack on extra weight to sustain them during the barren times ahead. Energetically, the autumn tide brings a thinning of the veil between worlds as we enter a time of both actual and symbolic death. Magic during autumn is focused on harvesting the literal and metaphorical fruits of our labors, preparing ourselves for the darker months, and communing with the spirits of our ancestors, who walk more freely during this time.

Winter Tide

As winter sets in with its increasingly long nights, the natural world slows down and closes its weary eyes. The plants and animals are tucked away, keeping themselves sheltered and warm as temperatures drop. With earlier sunsets and later sunrises, we find ourselves getting tired sooner and having a harder time getting out of bed in the morning. Energetically, the winter tide prompts us to rest and to be still, to turn inward and reflect. For it is in the darkness that we face our shadows and learn some of the deepest lessons about ourselves. The magic of winter is focused on introspection, protection from the gloom and the cold, as well as the coming together of family and the encouragement of health and prosperity in the New Year.

Spring Tide

Spring arrives with the return of the sun and the lengthening of days. After its long rest, the natural world gives a great yawn and a stretch. The plants slowly reemerge from the underground and the trees slowly begin to bud. The animals too come out from their winter hiding and become more active as the temperatures warm. Energetically, the spring tide brings a sense of hope and renewal. We open our windows to let in fresh air and clear out any remnants of the darker months behind us. Magic during the spring is focused on rebirth, cleansing, and planting the seeds of what we'd like to manifest in the coming year.

Summer Tide

During the summer months, the natural world is in its prime, pulsing with life and vibrant virtue. The budding plants of spring are now in full bloom and the trees stand full and verdant. The animals are at their most active, as are the spirits of the land. In particular, the Fair Folk are increasingly present during the warmer days. Energetically, the summer tide brings feelings of passion and joy as the sun reaches its zenith in the sky and we watch the seeds we planted earlier in the year come to fruition. Magic during the summer is focused on continued growth, success and completion, and love and friendship.

Sabbats: Seasonal Rituals and Celebrations

Due to our connection with the natural world and the way we are affected by the shifting seasonal tides, Witches have often made it a point to mark these changes with ritual and celebration. Today, many practitioners observe the *sabbats*—a set of seasonal holidays established amid the early development of Wicca in the 1950s. During this time, Gerald Gardner was highly influenced by the work of Egyptologist and writer Margaret Murray. In her book *The Witch-Cult in Western Europe*, Murray wrote extensively about the Witches' Sabbath, and it is likely her work that inspired Gardner to incorporate the concept into his practice, albeit using the French spelling *sabbat*. Gardner originally focused on the four dates as given by Murray, labeling them as November Eve, February Eve, May Eve, and August Eve. He equated these four sabbats with the four Celtic fire festivals, which he referred to as *Samhaim* (November 1), *Brigid* (February 1), *Bealteine* (May 1), and *Lughnasadh* (August 1).[98] These festivals are better known today as Samhain, Imbolc, Beltane, and Lammas. Gardner's coven did celebrate the solstices and equinoxes, but they were initially viewed as "lesser" and celebrated on the nearest full moon instead of on their actual date. However, this changed in 1958 when the coven requested that the solstices and equinoxes receive more attention and be celebrated on their

---

98. Gerald Gardner, *Witchcraft Today* (New York: Citadel Press, 2004), 130.

given date. Thus, the system of eight sabbats—which are collectively known today as the Wheel of the Year—was put forth.[99]

While the modern Wheel of the Year system is handy, to say the least, it is nonetheless based around one specific climate (i.e., Western European). Unfortunately, this means that as seasonal markers, the Sabbats may not align well with what's happening in other bioregions of the world. For example, not all places experience four distinct seasons, and even in those that do, the seasons may express themselves differently. Despite this, we seem to have become accustomed to a fixed system of seasonal rites that fall on specific calendar dates. Of course, one could also look at this issue from an astronomical perspective, that the solstices and equinoxes mark the beginning and ending of each season while the other four sabbats mark the points in between. However, even taking astronomy into consideration, these dates don't always reflect what's going on in a given region. For example, astronomically, the first day of winter occurs on December 21 (give or take), but the first snowfall where I live can happen as early as October. Additionally, when the spring equinox rolls around, it's a sure thing that we have at least two more months of snow left. Therefore, the question stands, if you're attempting to apply a fixed system of seasonal celebrations but it doesn't match what's happening in your local landscape, how well are you actually connecting to the natural world?

Reimagining the Wheel of the Year

If you've come to find that the Wheel of the Year doesn't align with the seasonal tides of your region, perhaps it's time to reimagine its structure. While this might seem quite radical in the face of the long-standing fixed system, remember that if you're trying to connect with the land, it's best to make that connection personal. The process of reimagining the Wheel of the Year is a twofold one in which you must first consider when exactly to celebrate a given sabbat and then what it is that you're celebrating. To begin, tune your awareness in to what is happening in the natural world around you throughout the year. How do you know when the seasons are changing? Are there specific signs that inform you that these changes are coming? Where I live, one of the signs that autumn has officially started is when the geese begin to migrate south. Likewise, I know spring is coming soon

---

99. Hutton, *Triumph of the Moon*, 248.

when the geese have started to return. Are there particular animals in your region that act as harbingers of the changing seasons?

Furthermore, consider the cycle of trees and other plants. What are the first plants to emerge after winter? When do the first buds on the trees appear? What about the weather? Look to the forecast to figure out when the first frost will arrive or when temperatures are predicted to rise. If you live in a climate where you don't experience snow or frost, are there other weather patterns that announce the coming and going of the seasons? I recommend recording these observations in your journal so that you can return to them later and see what patterns emerge over time. As you gain a clearer picture of how nature signals its seasonal changes, you can then determine when the best time is to hold your rituals and celebrations.

The second step is to consider what these times of year mean to you; in other words, what exactly are you celebrating? Some people are put off by the theme of agricultural fertility that is often attributed to the sabbats, viewing it as obsolete given that many of us are no longer directly dependent upon farming for survival. While it's true that today a large percentage of people are no longer farmers, we are all still connected to, and in some way dependent upon, the land. We eat food that comes from the earth, even if we aren't growing and harvesting it ourselves. We live upon the land, even if it's in an apartment building or a house that someone else built. We still experience the seasonal changes and weather patterns. And we still have relationships with the spirits of the land. Furthermore, the themes of agricultural fertility are many times used as metaphors for the psychological themes that are reflected in the seasons, spirits, and ourselves. For example, spring is the time when new plants sprout and fresh seeds are sown, the animals emerge from their winter slumber, and the sun begins to return to its full vibrancy in the sky. Even if we aren't planting crops or attending baby animals, we can still feel the energetic pull toward new beginnings and personal growth during this time of year.

There are many possible narratives for the sabbats, and it's important to find one that is personally relevant to both yourself and your landscape. Ask yourself, what is it that you feel during each season? What's your energy like, both physically and spiritually? As you consider your own internal seasonal shifts, what themes do you notice? How could you mindfully honor these changes with ritual and celebration? Also, think back to those signs from nature that you've recorded in your journal. Are there specific natural occurrences that hold particular meaning for you and that could be incorporated into a seasonal ritual and celebration?

EXERCISE 40:
Creating a Personal Seasonal Ritual

Purpose: To create a seasonal ritual based on the climate of your bioregion.

Location: A quiet space where you can think and write.

Time: Anytime.

Tools: Your journal and a pen.

In your journal, respond to the following questions:

+ What will be the focus of your seasonal ritual? What are the natural themes of your chosen seasonal tide? What are the common weather patterns during this time (snow, rain, heat, etc.)? What about the behavior of plants and animals (falling leaves, budding flowers, migration/hibernation)? What are the corresponding energetic themes of this time of year?

+ How will you be honoring these themes during your ritual? Will you be casting a spell, saying a prayer, giving offerings, meditating, crossing the hedge, etc.? Are there pre-established seasonal traditions or customs practiced by your family or cultural ancestors that you can incorporate into your ritual?

+ When will you perform your ritual? Is there a specific day or time when it should be done? Are there particular signs from the natural world that will inform you when it's time? Is there a particular calendar date that works best?

Once you've answered the questions above, it's time to weave your responses together in order to form your personal seasonal ritual. Plan for the day on which you'd like to perform your ritual and gather any magical tools or ingredients you might need. When the time comes, carry out your chosen ritual actions while concentrating on how they align your body, mind, and spirit with the seasonal rhythms of the natural world. No matter what your specific ritual entails, allow yourself to embrace and become one with the energetic current of the season, celebrating the turning tides and the magic that comes with such changes.

Weather

Humans are, in a sense, at the mercy of the weather, as it can have a major impact on us physically and emotionally. Physically, the weather determines what we are able to do when out of doors. Due to extreme temperatures or weather patterns like rain or heavy snow, we are often sequestered to our homes, where we can feel trapped or cooped up. Emotionally, the weather can elicit a variety of reactions. Sunny, warm days often bring a feeling of joy, while rainy overcast days often bring a sense of gloom and sadness. Then there are those extreme weather events such as tornadoes, droughts, and blizzards that cause us to feel anxious and afraid. Yet, instead of feeling powerless in the face of the different meteorological tides, Witches have an understanding of how to tap into and channel the power of the weather in order to achieve our magical intentions. Each form of weather has its own magical use, and there are countless ways to apply them in your own Craft.

Wind

Whether it's a soft breeze or a fearsome tempest, whenever the wind blows, change is never far behind. Magically speaking, wind can be used to carry our spells and prayers to their intended destinations. The wind, based on which direction it is heralding from, is charged with corresponding magical virtues:

North Wind (Cool/Dry): Binding, banishing, and hexing.

East Wind (Warm/Wet): Clarity, inspiration, and wisdom.

South Wind (Warm/Dry): Protection, love, courage.

West Wind (Cool/Wet): Healing, cleansing, intuition.

In order to determine which direction the wind is blowing from, try tying a length of ribbon to a tree branch high enough to catch the breeze. You'll be able to calculate the wind's origin based on the direction in which the ribbon moves. For example, if the ribbon is flapping toward the west, the current wind is an eastern one.

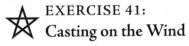

EXERCISE 41:
Casting on the Wind

Purpose: To cast a spell using the virtues of the wind.

Location: Outdoors, where you can directly experience the wind.

Time: A blustery day on which the wind is blowing from a direction that corresponds with your magical intention.

Tools: None.

Begin by holding your arms outstretched above your head, with fingers spread wide. Close your eyes and focus intently upon what you desire. Feel the wind as it moves through and around you; sense its magic mingling with your own. When you have sufficiently called to mind what you'd like to manifest, then speak, chant, or sing words of intention into the wind. Allow each word to leave your lips and be carried off on the breeze, knowing that the spirits of the wind will carry them where they need to go.

Rain

Rain is vital to many landscapes, as it replenishes and renews the earth, providing life-giving water to both plants and animals. For humans, rain can be just as restorative, as it energetically possesses healing and cleansing properties. Collecting rainwater can be a great way of accessing and utilizing the magical virtues of this particular type of weather. The next time there is a rain shower, place a jar or bowl outside for a couple of minutes. When you've collected enough water, bring the container inside. You can store the water away for later use, but I recommend using it sooner rather than later.

 FROM THE BLACK BOOK:
Rain Water Infusions for Healing and Cleansing

For both of these recipes you will need approximately 2 cups of fresh rain water. To begin, pour the water into a pot and bring to a low boil. Then, pour the boiling water into a bowl over the following herbal mixture of your choosing:

For healing: Chamomile, echinacea, and plantain.

For cleansing: Sage, rosemary, and vervain.

Allow the herbs to steep for at least 10 minutes before straining them out. You can add the healing infusion to a bath or apply it directly to areas of the body associated with sickness or injury. The cleansing infusion can be stored in a spray bottle and used to clean your home and certain magical items.

Thunder and Lightning

Thunderstorms are both physically and spiritually electrifying. The energy given off by thunder and lightning can be used to amplify any spell or ritual, as well as to charge magical items such as charms and talismans. If you have a particular spell that needs an extra magical boost, try casting it on a stormy night, allowing the thunder and lightning to punctuate your words and actions. Call out to the spirits of the storm, asking them to join you in your working. Reach out and take hold of the lightning and thunder's magical power, combining it with your own before projecting it toward your intended goal.

To charge magical items with the energy of thunder and lightning, start by setting the item upon your dish. Then, simply place the dish outside or on a windowsill where the item can absorb the storm's electrical virtue.

Snow and Ice

While other forms of weather—such as wind and lightning—have a fast-paced magical energy, snow and ice have the ability to slow things down. Scientifically, we know that when the molecules in water reach freezing point, they have slowed down enough to become solid. We can employ the virtues of snow and ice in our magical workings to halt problematic situations or even bind our enemies.

EXERCISE 42:
Binding with Snow and Ice

Purpose: To magically bind a harmful or otherwise problematic person.

Location: Indoors and outdoors.

Time: During the waning moon or on the night of a new moon.

Tools: A picture of the target and a bowl of snow (or a bowl of rainwater if you don't have snow in your bioregion).

To begin, obtain a picture of the individual and on the back write out their problematic behaviors that you'd like to see stop. If you have snow in your region, go out and collect a good amount in a bowl. If you don't have snow in your region, you can use collected rainwater. Next, bury the picture in snow or submerge it in rainwater before placing the bowl in your freezer. As you complete these actions, recite the following spell thrice:

With this spell I ice you out.
Your harmful actions become nowt.
I bury you within the frost,
So from my life, you'll now get lost.

Planets

Since the earliest days of humankind, we have looked toward the celestial heavens with awe. There truly is nothing quite like the experience of gazing up at the
blazing stars scattered across a clear night sky. As they are the most visible to the
naked eye, most people readily recognize the strong influence that both the sun
and moon have upon us. The other planets, though, have potent magical virtues
as well and can affect us just the same. Within magical traditions among the ancient world, practitioners worked with the seven classical planets—or those they
could observe in the sky during that time. The seven planets included the moon,
the sun, Mars, Mercury, Jupiter, Venus, and Saturn (Uranus, Neptune, and Pluto
were not discovered until 1781, 1846, and 1930, respectively). Today, Witches
can call upon these same seven classical planets to channel their magical virtues
toward spells and rituals. The specific magical number and magical virtues of
each planet are as follows:

Planet	Day of the Week	Number	Magical Virtues	Symbol
Moon	Monday	9	Psychic powers, dreams, emotional healing	☽
Mars	Tuesday	5	Protection, courage, strength	♂
Mercury	Wednesday	8	Communication, knowledge, travel	☿
Jupiter	Thursday	4	Abundance, business, good fortune	♃
Venus	Friday	7	Love, beauty, friendship	♀
Saturn	Saturday	3	Banishing, binding, hexing	♄
Sun	Sunday	6	Physical healing, growth, success	☉

Planetary Squares

Also known as *kameas*, planetary squares are the mathematical summation of a planet's magical virtue. Based on a series of mathematical computations, the numbers associated with each planet are organized into a specially created grid—or square. When employed in spellcraft, these squares are created as a means of channeling the power of a particular planet whose virtues align with the intention of the work at hand. To use a planetary square, you must first draw out the appropriately sized grid—which is determined based on each planet's associated magical number (3 × 3 for Saturn, 4 × 4 for Jupiter, 5 × 5 for Mars, 6 × 6 for the sun, 7 × 7 for Venus, 8 × 8 for mercury, and 9 × 9 for the moon). Then, focusing on invoking the planetary virtue, begin filling in the square in numerical order (use the pictures below as a guide). This will require a good deal of concentration, as you'll be jumping around the grid quite a bit. Once complete, the square can be used in a number of ways, such as being added to a charm-bag or placed beneath a hallowed candle.

37	78	29	70	21	62	13	54	5
6	38	79	30	71	22	63	14	46
47	7	39	80	31	72	23	55	15
16	48	8	40	81	32	64	24	56
57	17	49	9	41	73	33	65	25
26	58	18	50	1	42	74	34	66
67	27	59	10	51	2	43	75	35
36	68	19	60	11	52	3	44	76
77	28	69	20	61	12	53	4	45

Moon Planetary Square

11	24	7	20	3
4	12	25	8	16
17	5	13	21	9
10	18	1	14	22
23	6	19	2	15

Mars Planetary Square

8	58	59	5	4	62	63	1
49	15	14	52	53	11	10	56
41	23	22	44	45	19	18	48
32	34	35	29	28	38	39	25
40	26	27	37	36	30	31	33
17	47	46	20	21	43	42	24
9	55	54	12	13	51	50	16
64	2	3	61	60	6	7	57

Mercury Planetary Square

4	14	15	1
9	7	6	12
5	11	10	8
16	2	3	13

Jupiter Planetary Square

22	47	16	41	10	35	4
5	23	48	17	42	11	29
30	6	24	49	18	36	12
13	31	7	25	43	19	37
38	14	32	1	26	44	20
21	39	8	33	2	27	45
46	15	40	9	34	3	28

Venus Planetary Square

4	9	2
3	5	7
8	1	6

Saturn Planetary Square

6	32	3	34	35	1
7	11	27	28	8	30
19	14	16	15	23	24
18	20	22	21	17	13
25	29	10	9	26	12
36	5	33	4	2	31

Sun Planetary Square[100]

Planetary Days and Hours

Each of the seven planets is linked to one of the seven days of the week. Monday is ruled by the moon, Tuesday by Mars, Wednesday by Mercury, Thursday by Jupiter, Friday by Venus, Saturday by Saturn, and Sunday by the sun. Additionally, each planet corresponds to particular hours—both a.m. and p.m.—on each given day. Starting at 1 a.m., the first hour of the day is associated with its ruling planet (e.g., the first hour of Sunday is associated with the sun). From there, the hours are determined using what is known as the Chaldean Order, or the sequence of planets from farthest to the closest in relation to the earth: Saturn, Jupiter, Mars, the sun, Venus, Mercury, and then the moon. The pattern continues throughout the day, ending at midnight. If you don't wish to calculate the hours in your head, you can make use of the charts on the next page.

When preparing for magical work, consider the planetary days and hours, which can be used to add extra power to your spells and rituals. For example, if you were planning to do a spell for healing a broken heart, you might want to perform it on a Monday (for the moon and emotional healing) and in the hour of Venus (for matters of the heart). The energy of the day's ruling planet tends to be more dominant than that of the particular hour. Therefore, I recommend that you match the planets according to which energy is needed more intensely.

---

100. Henry Cornelius Agrippa, *Three Books of Occult Philosophy*, trans. James Freake, ed. Donald Tyson (St. Paul, MN: Llewellyn Publications, 1993), 321–27.

Hour	Sun	Mon	Tue	Wed	Thu	Fri	Sat
1	☉	☽	♂	☿	♃	♀	♄
2	♀	♄	☉	☽	♂	☿	♃
3	☿	♃	♀	♄	☉	☽	♂
4	☽	♂	☿	♃	♀	♄	☉
5	♄	☉	☽	♂	☿	♃	♀
6	♃	♀	♄	☉	☽	♂	☿
7	♂	☿	♃	♀	♄	☉	☽
8	☉	☽	♂	☿	♃	♀	♄
9	♀	♄	☉	☽	♂	☿	♃
10	☿	♃	♀	♄	☉	☽	♂
11	☽	♂	☿	♃	♀	♄	☉
12	♄	☉	☽	♂	☿	♃	♀

A.M. Planetary Hour Chart

Hour	Sun	Mon	Tue	Wed	Thu	Fri	Sat
1	♃	♀	♄	☉	☽	♂	☿
2	♂	☿	♃	♀	♄	☉	☽
3	☉	☽	♂	☿	♃	♀	♄
4	♀	♄	☉	☽	♂	☿	♃
5	☿	♃	♀	♄	☉	☽	♂
6	☽	♂	☿	♃	♀	♄	☉
7	♄	☉	☽	♂	☿	♃	♀
8	♃	♀	♄	☉	☽	♂	☿
9	♂	☿	♃	♀	♄	☉	☽
10	☉	☽	♂	☿	♃	♀	♄
11	♀	♄	☉	☽	♂	☿	♃
12	☿	♃	♀	♄	☉	☽	♂

P.M. Planetary Hour Chart[101]

---

101. Agrippa, *Three Books of Occult Philosophy*, 372.

The Moon

Out of the seven classical planets, it is the moon in particular that has had a long-standing connection to the powers of Witchcraft and magic. Canidia, a Witch appearing in the writings of Horace, was credited with the power to "pluck the moon from heaven" using her spells.[102] Meanwhile, Witches in the Shetland Islands were said to dedicate themselves to the Devil by going to a beach at midnight on a full moon, placing their left hand under the soles of their feet and their right on the top of their head, then saying aloud, "The muckel maister Deil tak what's atween dis twa haunds!"[103] And who could forget the evocative words of Aradia as she taught her followers the ways of Witchcraft:

> *Whenever ye have need of anything,*
> *Once in a month, and when the moon is full,*
> *Ye shall assemble in some desert place,*
> *Or in a forest all together join...*[104]

We've already seen how the moon can aid in the magical planting and harvesting of herbs, but it can also help broadly in the working of magic spells and rituals. While the moon technically has eight phases, its magical tides can be generalized into four: the waxing moon, full moon, waning moon, and new moon. Much like the spring tide of the solar year, the waxing moon is a time of active growth and expansion. The waxing moon carries the virtues of new beginnings, and its powers can be channeled to help as we work toward reaching our goals. The full moon brings blessings and fulfillment as our goals are made manifest. It's a time of potent magic, when Witches channel the moon's powers to grant us our deepest desires. As the moon wanes, we enter a time of progressive decay and contraction similar to that of the autumn tide. The waning moon carries the virtues of endings and helps us to begin the process of letting go of that which no longer serves us. Finally, the new moon possesses the power of banishment, binding, and hexing.

---

102. Horace, *The Complete Odes and Epodes*, trans. David West (New York: Oxford University Press, 2008), 22.

103. Biot Edmondston and Jessie M. E. Saxby, *The Home of a Naturalist* (London: James Nisbet, 1888), 206, https://catalog.hathitrust.org/Record/100424072.

104. Charles Godfrey Leland, *Aradia: Gospel of the Witches* (London: Davit Nutt, 1899; repr., Glastonbury, UK: The Lost Library, 2012), 6.

It's a time of darkness and inward reflections, when Witches call upon the moon to aid us in our more shadowy workings.

⬟ EXERCISE 43:
Full Moon Blessing Ritual

Purpose: To channel the virtues of the full moon to manifest blessings in your life.

Location: Outdoors where there is a clear view of the moon or indoors in a quiet and comfortable space.

Time: The night of a full moon.

Tools: Compass-laying tools (pillar candle, a bowl of water, a bowl of dirt, incense, and your stang), your cauldron, your knife, and a white taper candle.

To begin, travel to your chosen location. When you've arrived, start by laying a compass using the Simple Compass-Laying Ritual on page 61. Afterward, place the cauldron in the center and the stang at the northern edge of the space.

Next, sit before the cauldron and, using your knife, carve words or symbols of intention upon the surface of the white taper candle. As you do so, visualize the manifestation of your desires. Once completed, lick your right thumb and then run it over your carvings, sealing it with your magical essence. Hold it aloft in the moonlight while reciting the following blessing:

> *I call upon the full moon this night,*
> *To hallow my candle burning bright,*
> *That it may help me to acquire*
> *All the things that I desire.*

Place the candle within the cauldron (you may need to melt the bottom of the candle before sticking it to the bottom of the cauldron). Take the remaining water from laying the compass and pour just enough of it into the cauldron to line the bottom before lighting the candle. Finally, starting in the north and moving clockwise, begin treading the mill. As you pace the compass, use the candle as your focal point, focusing on channeling the moon's virtues to assist you in manifesting your desires. Once you've reached a magical climax, stop in your tracks and project your power forth.

When you wish to end the ritual, dismantle the compass by walking the circumference of the space counterclockwise, starting in the north. As you walk, speak your words of gratitude and farewell to each of the directions as well as to the Witch Father and Witch Mother, spirits of the land, and your ancestors. Finish by pulling the stang up from the ground and cleaning your working space. Pour out the water from the cauldron on the ground and take the candle home. Continue lighting it over the next week, spending a few moments staring into the candle's flame and envisioning your wishes being fulfilled. Repeat this process each night until the candle has completely burnt out.

EXERCISE 44:
New Moon Banishing Ritual

Purpose: To channel the virtues of the new moon to banish unwanted influences from your life.

Location: Outdoors or indoors in a quiet and comfortable space.

Time: The night of a new moon.

Tools: Compass-laying tools (pillar candle, a bowl of water, a bowl of dirt, incense, and your stang), your cauldron, your knife, and a black taper candle.

To begin, travel to your chosen location. When you've arrived, start by laying a compass using the Simple Compass-Laying Ritual on page 61. Afterward, place the cauldron in the center and the stang at the northern edge of the space.

Next, sit before the cauldron and, using your knife, carve words or symbols of intention upon the surface of the black taper candle. As you do so, visualize that which you wish to banish from your life. Once completed, lick your right thumb and then run it over your carvings, sealing it with your magical essence. Hold it aloft in the moonlight while reciting the following banishing:

> *I call upon the new moon this night*
> *To hallow my candle burning bright,*

That it may banish from my life
All the things that cause me strife.

Place the candle within the cauldron (you may need to melt the bottom of the candle before sticking it to the bottom of the cauldron). Take the remaining water from laying the compass and pour just enough of it into the cauldron to line the bottom before lighting the candle. Finally, starting in the north and moving counterclockwise, begin treading the mill. As you pace the compass, use the candle as your focal point, channeling the moon's virtue to assist you in banishing that which no longer serves you. Once you've reached a magical climax, stop in your tracks and project your power forth.

When you wish to end the ritual, dismantle the compass by walking the circumference of the space counterclockwise, starting in the north. As you walk, speak your words of gratitude and farewell to each of the directions as well as to the Witch Father and Witch Mother, spirits of the land, and your ancestors. Finish by pulling the stang up from the ground and cleaning your working space. Pour out the water from the cauldron on the ground and take the candle home. Continue lighting it over the next week, spending a few moments staring into the candle's flame and envisioning the banishment of that which no longer serves you. Repeat this process each night until the candle has completely burnt out.

FROM THE SPIRITS OF LORE:
The Witches of Mid Calder

From the spirits of lore, there is a Scottish story that highlights the intimate relationship Witches have with the moon. As it goes, in the year 1582 Pope Gregory XIII introduced the Gregorian calendar as a replacement for the earlier Julian model. The new system had corrected the miscalculations of the previous one, which were made in regard to the length of the solar year. As part of the changes made within the new system, the date of the New Year was shifted from March 25 to January 1. However, many regions were resistant to this change. For example, it would be eighteen years before Scotland finally adopted the new calendar date. It was said that the Witches of Mid Calder of all people were especially displeased with the alterations. They were afraid that because of the changes being made to the calendar, the moon would become confused and lose her proper course through the night sky. The Witches feared that eventually the moon would cease to appear at all. Thus, it became local legend that every twenty-eight days, the Witches of Mid Calder would fly up into the sky and help keep their beloved moon on track by guiding her movements.[105]

---

105. Jennifer Westwood and Sophia Kingshill, *The Lore of Scotland: A Guide to Scottish Legends* (London: Random House UK, 2009), 264.

Part V
Reflecting on the Crooked Path

Emerging from the forest, you continue walking along the path as it cuts through an expansive, open field. You can see that the path stretches far into the distance, seemingly going on forever. In the west, the sun is sinking below the horizon while the full moon starts its ascent into the sky. You can sense that you are on the precipice of something life altering. You've traveled a long way and you've learned so many new things. You know how to perform rituals and cast spells, how to commune with spirits and travel into the Otherworld, and how to connect with and wield the power of the natural world. Looking back at the road behind you, you feel a sense of pride and accomplishment. Turning forward and walking a bit further, you find an altar standing in the middle of the road, a stang topped with a burning candle between its tines. You understand that this is a milestone, a sign that you've reached a significant point in your journey. In your heart you know that it's time to decide whether or not to officially dedicate yourself to the Crooked Path.

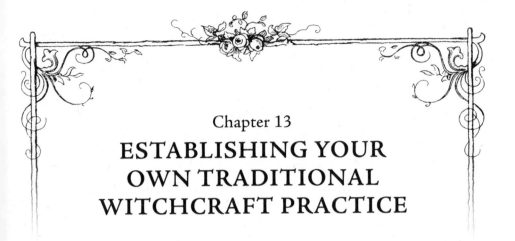

Chapter 13

ESTABLISHING YOUR OWN TRADITIONAL WITCHCRAFT PRACTICE

Here you are, at the end of this book. You've come a long way on your journey, crossing great distances through these pages. You've learned about history and folklore, performed rituals and cast spells, taken flight into the Otherworld, met with a number of spirits, and connected with the powers of the natural world around you. The road has been long, and there is still much further to go if you choose to continue on its serpentine course. But before deciding upon where you'll go from here, take a moment now to rest and reflect on the path that you've been walking. Call to mind where you've been and all those new things, the beliefs and practices, you've discovered along the way. After doing so, you might realize that Traditional Witchcraft is not the path for you, in which case I encourage you to continue exploring until you find one that feels like the right fit. However, if you've come to find that you feel at home within the pages of this book and that you'd like to keep exploring the ways of Traditional Witchcraft, then I welcome you to take the final steps—organizing your personal practice, formulating your Witch's pact, and dedicating yourself to the Crooked Path.

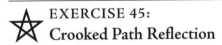 ## EXERCISE 45:
Crooked Path Reflection

Purpose: To reflect upon what you've learned along the Crooked Path thus far.

Location: A quiet space where you can think and write.

Time: Anytime.

Tools: Your journal and a pen.

In your journal, respond to the following questions:

+ Now that you've reached the end of this book, how would you personally define Traditional Witchcraft?

+ If you had any preconceived notions about Traditional Witchcraft, have they changed? And if so, how?

+ Of the tools discussed, which is your favorite? How do you prefer to use them within your magical workings?

+ Of the rituals discussed in chapter 5, was there one you resonated with more so than the others? Was there one you didn't find all that useful?

+ How would you change or alter it to better suit your personal style?

+ How can you personalize and adapt folk spells and charms to fit the modern context of your life?

+ What are your thoughts on the Witch Father and Witch Mother? Do you feel called to work with gods in your personal path? Why or why not?

+ Who are the ancestors you wish to honor and work with in your Craft?

+ Have you met a familiar spirit? If so, what is your relationship like and how do you benefit from one another?

+ How do you relate to your fetch spirit? Is there a certain way you communicate or work?

+ What kinds of offerings do you give to your spirits? When and how often do you give these offerings?

+ What does the Otherworld—including the Upperworld, Midworld, and Underworld—look like to you?

+ Are there specific tools that you find helpful when hedge-crossing?

+ Why do you think bioregionalism is important in the practice of Traditional Witchcraft?

+ What are some of the plants native to your area and how can you use them in your Craft?

+ How can you make use of native stones?

- What signs have you started to notice from the animals of your local landscape?

- How do you personally align with the seasonal tides? In what ways can you mark these yearly shifts in the natural world?

- In what ways can you incorporate weather patterns into your Craft? Are there particular types of weather that you connect with more so than others?

- What role do the planets play in your practice? How do you relate to them and how can you make use of their magical virtues?

Daily and Occasional Magical Practices

Taking into consideration your responses to the above questions, how can you apply what you've learned into a workable practice? In other words, how can you establish a semi-structured routine for practicing Traditional Witchcraft? Having a routine is helpful because it keeps us connected to our spirits and assists us in growing our abilities as Witches. However, it's important not to be too structured, as this can cause us to become rigid and inflexible, inadvertently stifling our magical creativity. There is sometimes a belief that in order to be an authentic Witch, you must be living in a constant flux of rituals and spells. You must be actively performing acts of Witchcraft at all times, lest you be disenchanted and mundane. Yet magic is whatever we make it. Witchcraft is more than a set of particular practices: it's a state of mind, something that lives in our hearts and permeates all we do—even the most mundane of acts.

When it comes to structure and routine, I find that it's helpful to think in terms of practices that are daily and those that are occasional. Daily practices typically include attending our spirits through communication and offerings. As such, you might begin your day by pouring a cup of coffee for your ancestors or speaking with the land wights on your walk to work. You might leave out a bowl of honey for the Fair Folk or end your night by expressing gratitude to the Witch Father and Witch Mother. Magically speaking, you might carry a charm-bag in your pocket for healing or repeat a chant for promoting a sense of calm during a stressful day. You might light a candle to increase concentration when studying for an exam or recite a spell for protection while driving. These are all examples of simple ways you can practice your Craft each day. I recommend finding at least two small acts of Witchcraft that you can engage in every day.

Then there are those practices that are best carried out occasionally, including rituals like the compass round, treading the mill, and the housel. While you could theoretically perform these rituals every day, doing so would require you (and your spirits) to expend an exhausting amount of magical energy. The same is true for the practice of hedge-crossing, which, as we've discussed previously, can have detrimental effects if done too often. Therefore, you would do well to reserve these practices for biweekly or monthly occasions. I recommend using the phases of the moon to allocate when to perform rituals. For example, I will typically tread the mill on the night of a full moon and cross the hedge on the night of a new moon.

Covens and Community

As a part of your continuing journey, you may wish to find a group, or coven to practice your Craft with. There are many benefits to coven work, including a sense of community and solidarity. Covens are often experienced as a type of family in which members can rely on one another for support and guidance. The Crooked Path can be a lonely one at times and it's nice to have someone to walk with, even if just for a while. There are also magical benefits to working in a coven, namely that having more people means being able to create more power. Covens are capable of generating an incredible amount of magical energy for spells and rituals.

However, finding an established coven of Traditional Witches can prove to be difficult. Traditional Witchcraft covens tend to be exceedingly private and less likely to advertise than covens belonging to other traditions. That being said, if you truly desire to join a coven there are a few ways you might reasonably find one. I recommend attending local events, such as a Pagan Pride Day or open ritual. While these events may not be your exact flavor, you are more apt to find someone of like mind the more you interact with the local Witchcraft community. If you are lucky enough to have a nearby occult shop, check to see what classes they may be offering or get to know the staff—they may have leads on local groups. Additionally, you will want to check online—I recommend The Witches' Voice, a website dedicated entirely to Witchcraft resources, including covens and groups listed by country, state, and city.[106]

---

106. www.witchvox.com.

Be aware that not all covens are created equally. For a coven to work—both magically and interpersonally—there must be a balance of mutual trust and respect among its members. Unfortunately, this is not always the case, and there are some groups that become unhealthy and dysfunctional for a variety of reasons, including power struggles and coercive behavior. When approaching a potential coven, use your intuition and common sense to assess for possible red flags. For example, you should never have to pay to belong to a coven (outside of chipping in for ritual materials like candles or incense). Most importantly, though, you should never have to do anything that compromises your health, safety, or personal ethics. While covens commonly have structure or hierarchy, this does not mean that you must sacrifice your own autonomy. Don't be afraid of seeking out a coven, because there are plenty of healthy and positive ones out there. But don't settle for a coven simply because it seems like the only one available to you. It is better to continue the search than to become entangled with an abusive group.

In addition to, or in place of, physical covens, you might want to consider online resources and groups, which can offer similar support and guidance. There are Facebook groups and other forum-style websites completely dedicated to the practice of Traditional Witchcraft. Through these sites you will be able to interact with Traditional Witches from all over the world—to exchange ideas, share experiences, and bolster one another in your Craft. While it may not be quite the same experience as having a physical coven, don't underestimate the power of the internet to bring people together. I've met many of my Witch friends online, and although we haven't met in person, we still have developed close bonds. Depending upon where you live, you may feel isolated from other Witches. In this case, the internet can be an invaluable source of community connection.

EXERCISE 46:
Formulating a Witch's Pact

Purpose: To consider your intentions moving forward as a Traditional Witch and to create a pact, pledging yourself to the Crooked Path.

Location: A quiet space where you can think and write.

Time: Anytime.

Tools: A piece of paper, a pen, and a disposable lancet (optional).

To begin, reflect upon the following questions, taking time to meditate on each one before writing out your answers out on a piece of paper.

+ What does it mean to you to be a Traditional Witch? What sort of traits must you have? Do you have these traits already or do you need to work on developing them?

+ What can you offer the world as a Traditional Witch? How can you be of service to yourself, to others, and to the natural world?

+ How will you stay true to yourself, to your spirits, and to your Craft?

+ What do you wish to let go of as you move forward on your journey along the Crooked Path? Do you have any fears that are holding you back? How can you work to release them?

+ What do you wish to manifest in your life as you continue on this path?

When you've finished recording your answers, carefully review everything that you've written. Make sure you've expressed your thoughts and feelings nice and clearly, with true intent behind each word. Next, sign your name at the bottom of the page. Finally, carefully draw blood from your left thumb and press it into the paper, sealing the pact. Be safe! Use a sterile single-use diabetic lancet and wash your hands afterward. If for whatever reason you can't use blood, use a drop of your spit instead. After sealing the pact, tuck the paper away in a safe place until you are ready to perform the following dedication ritual.

✪ EXERCISE 47: A Traditional Witch's Dedication Ritual

Purpose: To dedicate yourself to the practice of Traditional Witchcraft

Location: Outdoors in a wild and desolate place.

Time: Midnight on a full moon.

Tools: Compass-laying tools (pillar candle, a bowl of water, a bowl of dirt, incense, and your stang), your cauldron, your signed pact, and a taper candle (white or black in color).

To begin, prepare the space by laying a compass using the Simple Compass-Laying Ritual on page 61. Place the cauldron on the ground at the foot of the stang. Ground yourself in the space, tuning in to the energy of the land. Become aware of the liminality within the compass round, with the roadways into the Otherworld opened. When you feel connected, call out to your spirit allies, informing them of your intent to dedicate yourself to the path of Traditional Witchcraft. Then, complete the following steps:

1. Stand before the stang, holding the lit taper candle between its tines.

2. Using the candle's flame, ignite your paper. Let it burn for a moment before dropping it into the cauldron to be safely consumed by the flames.

3. Next, kneel before the stang. Place your left hand under the soles of your feet and your right hand on top of your head. Then, focusing your intentions, recite the following declaration:

Spirits, please hear me on this night,
As I sacrifice my old self and all that holds me back
So that I may be reborn as a Witch.
And as such, I now pledge everything between by my two hands
To thee and to my Craft!

Remain in that stance for a few moments, giving the spirits time to approach you and speak their words of wisdom. Once they have finished, stand before the stang and give thanks to the spirits for witnessing your rite and bestowing you with their blessings. Finally, when you wish to end the ritual, dismantle the compass and walk the circumference of the space counterclockwise, starting in the north. As you walk, speak your words of gratitude and farewell to each of the directions as well as to the Witch Father and Witch Mother, spirits of the land, and your ancestors. Finish by pulling the stang up from the ground and cleaning up your working space.

Conclusion

Feeling a sense of overwhelming pride, you step around the altar and back onto the dirt path. Overhead the full moon shines so bright that the entire field is illuminated. To your left you spot a group of deer standing peacefully in the tall grass while the glow of a hundred fireflies fills the air around you. You can sense the change that has occurred within yourself, you feel awakened to a new reality. Everywhere you look, you see spirits and magic, in the stars, in the trees, in the bats fluttering across the sky. Additionally, you can feel the comforting presence of the Witch Father and Witch Mother, your ancestors, and your familiar spirit as they walk alongside you. And as you continue to move forward on the Crooked Path, you know in your heart that you are home.

A WITCH'S FAREWELL

So now you're ready. Free to continue your journey on the Crooked Path. You've completed all the foundational work and now you must grab your broomstick and fly. Now is the time to take what you've learned and go get your hands dirty, to grow from experience. I have poured my heart and soul into this book and I hope that you've found it to be helpful, whether you're just starting or have been on this path for a while now. As I stated in the introduction, my goal in writing this book was to create a down-to-earth guide to Traditional Witchcraft, one that cuts through the unnecessary pomp and gets right into the practical methods for working magic, connecting with the Otherworld, and relating to the natural world.

My wish for you, as you go forward on your individual path, is that you will have access to the magic both within yourself and without, that the way into the Otherworld will always be open to you, and that you will have a lasting relationship with your local landscape. And so, with that, I will leave you with three last bits of wisdom that I hope you will take with you no matter where you end up:

+ Traditional Witchcraft should be a personal experience, infused with the traditions and folklore of your ancestors and the magical virtues of your natural landscape.
+ There is no right or wrong way to practice Traditional Witchcraft, so long as it works for you.
+ Authenticity in Traditional Witchcraft comes from having confidence in yourself, from having personal connection with the spirits, and from magic that gets results.

GLOSSARY

Altar: A surface that has been dedicated for the purposes of working magic and communing with spirits.

Ancestors: A group of human spirits with whom one has had close bonds—includes familial ancestors, land-based ancestors, and the Mighty Dead.

Axis Mundi: The cosmic axis, or world tree, upon which the three realms are centered.

Azazel: One of the chief Watchers who taught humans the art of forging weapons and using makeup and other personal adornments.

Baba Yaga: A Witch from Russian folklore who lives in a house upon chicken feet, surrounded by a fence topped with skulls filled with divine fire.

Baneful: Relating to harm or being harmful.

Banishing: The act of magically expelling or doing away with something or someone.

Banshee: A type of faerie who has a wailing cry that warns of an impending death.

Binding: The act of magically restraining or incapacitating something or someone.

Brownie: A type of faerie that lives within the home and completes chores while the inhabitants are asleep.

Cailleach: An Irish and Scottish goddess of the land and weather.

Charm-Bag: A type of charm created by filling a cloth pouch with different items, such as herbs and stones that contain virtues corresponding to one's magical intention.

Compass Round: A ritually created, liminal working space in which Traditional Witches work magic and navigate the Otherworld.

Coven: A group of Witches who practice their Craft together, often led by a Magister, a Maiden, or both.

Cunning Folk: Early magical practitioners in the British Isles who often worked to detect harmful Witches and reverse their baneful magic.

Curse: The act of magically causing long-term or permanent harm.

Elfame: A Scottish term for the faerie realm.

Familiar Spirit: An umbrella term that refers to a spirit who comes to the aid of a Witch, often appearing in animal form.

Fetch: A part of the Witch's soul that is associated with the Underworld and can be sent out—often in animal form—to complete various magical tasks.

Flying Ointment: A balm created from entheogenic herbs that, when applied to the body, helps facilitate hedge-crossing.

Genius Loci: The spirit of a place who guards the specific area of land.

Glamoury: The act of magically changing the appearance of someone or something.

Green Man: A foliate face that adorns old churches, often interpreted as a facet of the Witch Father as the King of the Wildwood.

Hagstone: A rock with a naturally occurring hole through its center, thought to have a number of magical virtues, including protection and luck.

Hallow: The act of magically cleansing, blessing, or otherwise imbuing an object with magical power.

Hecate: The Greek goddess of the crossroads and Witchcraft.

Hedge-Crossing: The process of venturing outside of one's body and traveling in spirit form into the Otherworld.

Hex: The act of magically causing temporary or short-term harm.

Holda: A Germanic goddess of birth, death, spinning, and Witchcraft.

Housel: A ritual of thanksgiving, communion, and blessings in which the spirits are given offerings, typically of bread and wine.

Land Wight: The spirits of nature who inhabit the plants, rocks, and other natural objects.

Lucifer: A fallen angel or a light-bearing god; another guise of the Witch Father.

Magister: The masculine leader of a coven.

Magistra: The feminine leader of a coven. Also called a Maiden.

Maiden: See *Magistra*.

Man in Black: Another name for the Witch Father, particularly associated with his presence at the Sabbath.

Midworld: The physical world of humans as well as the hidden landscape behind it, which is inhabited by spirits such as the Fair Folk.

Mighty Dead: A group of ancestors made up of Witches and other magical practitioners who have passed on.

Moirai: The three Fates from Greek mythology, composed of Clotho, Lachesis, and Atropa.

Nicnevin: A Scottish goddess of Witchcraft and magic.

Otherworld: The world of spirits, divided into three realms—the Upperworld, Midworld, and Underworld.

Poppet: A magical doll used to represent the target of a spell or ritual.

Redcap: A type of malevolent faerie known to throw rocks at the heads of humans.

Sabbat: A modern ritual celebration marking the changing of the seasons. See also *Wheel of the Year*.

Sabbath: A nocturnal meeting of Witches and spirits occurring in the Otherworld.

Shapeshifting: The magical act of changing one's spirit form into the guise of an animal.

Stang: A bifurcated ritual staff that is used as an altar to the Witch Father and to direct magical power.

Traditional Witchcraft: An umbrella term that covers a vast array of non-Wiccan practices that are inspired by folklore. These practices may be viewed as religious or spiritual depending upon the group or individual practitioner. Traditional Witches focus on the use of magic, connecting with the natural landscape, and working with various spirits in both the physical realm and the Otherworld.

Treading the Mill: A ritual involving repetitive circling around a fixed central object with one's head turned to the side and slightly tilted back; used to alter consciousness and raise personal magical power.

Tubal Cain: A biblical figure, the first blacksmith; venerated by some as an aspect of the Witch Father.

Underworld: The lower realm of the Otherworld, where the ancestors reside. Often associated with the powers of emotions.

Upperworld: The upper realm of the Otherworld, where the gods reside. Often associated with the powers of the mind.

Virtue: The magical powers contained within natural objects, such as plants, stones, animals, planets, and so on.

Watchers: A group of fallen angels who taught humans different skills, including the use of sorcery, herbs, and astrology, and how to interpret the signs of the earth.

Wheel of the Year: A modern system of seasonal ritual celebrations made up of eight sabbats: Samhain, the winter solstice (Yule), Imbolc, the spring equinox (Ostara), Beltane, the summer solstice (Litha), Lammas, and the fall equinox (Mabon).

Wicca: A specific subset of Witchcraft founded by Gerald Gardner during the late 1940s and early 1950s.

Wild Hunt: A retinue of ghosts, faeries, and other beings who are said to take to the sky on stormy nights, collecting the souls of the dead and warning of impending disasters.

Witch Bottle: A type of protective and anti-hexing charm that involves filling a jar with sharp objects (e.g., pins, needles, and nails) and urine.

Witch Father: The archetypal masculine deity within Traditional Witchcraft.

Witch Mother: The archetypal feminine deity within Traditional Witchcraft.

World Tree: See *axis mundi.*

BIBLIOGRAPHY

Agrippa, Henry Cornelius. *Three Books of Occult Philosophy*. Translated by James Freake. Edited by Donald Tyson. St. Paul, MN: Llewellyn Publications, 1993.

Apuleius. *The Golden Ass*. Translated by Robert Graves. New York: Farrar, Straus and Giroux, 2009.

Beyerl, Paul. *The Master Book of Herbalism*. Blaine, WA: Phoenix Publishing, 1984.

Bible. King James Version. Peabody, MA: Hendrickson Publishers, 2011.

Black, G. F., and Northcote W. Thomas. *Examples of Printed Folk-lore Concerning the Orkney & Shetland Islands*. London: David Nutt, 1903. https://catalog.hathitrust.org/Record/001648704.

Bottrell, William. *Traditions and Hearthside Stories of West Cornwall*. Vol. 1. Penzance, UK: W. Cornish, 1870. Electronic reproduction by John Bruno Hare for the Internet Sacred Text Archive. https://www.sacred-texts.com/neu/celt/swc1/index.htm.

Boyer, Corinne. *Under the Witching Tree*. London: Troy Books Publishing, 2016.

Brand, John. *Observations on Popular Antiquities*. London: Chatto and Windus, 1877. https://catalog.hathitrust.org/Record/102427510.

Carmichael, Alexander. *The Carmina Gadelica*. Vol. 2. Edinburgh, UK: T. and A. Constable, 1900. https://books.google.com/books?id=duMOAAAAQAAJ.

Cheney, Ednah Dow. *Stories of the Olden Times*. Boston, MA: Lee and Shepard, 1890. https://catalog.hathitrust.org/Record/100558500.

Cochrane, Robert. "Letter Thirteen." In *The Robert Cochrane Letters: An Insight into Modern Traditional Witchcraft*, edited by Michael Howard. Somerset, UK: Capall Bann Publishing, 2003.

———. "Letter Three." In *The Robert Cochrane Letters: An Insight into Modern Traditional Witchcraft*, edited by Michael Howard. Somerset: Capall Bann Publishing, 2002.

———. "Letter Two." In *The Robert Cochrane Letters: An Insight into Modern Traditional Witchcraft*, edited by Michael Howard. Somerset: Capall Bann Publishing, 2002.

———. "Witchcraft Today." In *The Roebuck in the Thicket: An Anthology of the Robert Cochrane Witchcraft Tradition*, edited by Michael Howard. Somerset: Capall Bann Publishing, 2001.

Cromek, Robert Hartley, Allan Cunningham, and William Gillespie. *Remains of Nithsdale and Galloway Song*. London: T. Cadell and W. Davies, 1810. https://books.google.com/books/about/Remains_of_Nithsdale_and_Galloway_Song_w.html?id=FdxiAAAAcAAJ.

Cummer, Veronica, ed. *To Fly by Night*. Los Angeles, CA: Pendraig Publishing, 2010.

Cunningham, Scott. *Earth Power*. St. Paul, MN: Llewellyn Publications, 1983.

Davidson, Thomas. *Rowan Tree & Red Thread*. Edinburgh: Oliver and Boyd, 1949.

Davies, Owen. *Popular Magic*. London: Hambledon Continuum, 2003.

Davis, Hubert J. *American Witch Stories*. Middle Village, NY: Jonathan David Publishers, 1990.

Edmondston, Biot, and Jessie M. E. Saxby. *The Home of a Naturalist*. London: James Nisbet, 1888. https://catalog.hathitrust.org/Record/100424072.

Farrar, Janet, and Stewart Farrar. *The Witches' Bible*. Custer, WA: Phoenix Publishing, 1996.

Forbes, William. *The Institutes of the Law of Scotland*. Edinburgh, UK: John Mosman and Co., 1730. https://books.google.com/books?id=DTdcAAAAQAAJ.

Gardner, Gerald. *The Meaning of Witchcraft*. York Beach, ME: Weiser, 2004.

———. *Witchcraft Today.* Fiftieth anniversary edition. New York: Citadel Press, 2004.

Gary, Gemma. *The Black Toad.* London: Troy Books, 2012.

———. *The Charmers' Psalter.* London: Troy Books, 2014.

———. *The Devil's Dozen.* London: Troy Books, 2015.

———. *Traditional Witchcraft: A Cornish Book of Ways.* London: Troy Books, 2011.

Ginzburg, Carlo. *Ecstasies: Deciphering the Witches' Sabbath.* New York: Pantheon Books, 1991.

Gowdin, Kerriann, ed. *The Museum of Witchcraft: A Magical History.* Bodmin, UK: The Occult Art Company and the Friends of the Bodcastle Museum of Witchcraft, 2011.

Goss, K. David. *Documents of the Salem Witch Trials.* Santa Barbara, CA: ABC-CLIO, 2018.

Grieve, Maud. *A Modern Herbal.* Vol. 1. Mineola, NY: Dover Publications, 1971.

———. *A Modern Herbal.* Vol. 2. Mineola, NY: Dover Publications, 1971.

Hansen, Harold A. *The Witch's Garden.* Santa Cruz, CA: Unity Press, 1978.

Harland, John, and Thomas Turner Wilkinson. *Lancashire Folk-lore.* London: Frederick Warne and Co., 1867. https://archive.org/details/lancashire folklo00harl/page/n4.

Hatsis, Thomas. *The Witches' Ointment.* Rochester, VT: Park Street Press, 2015.

Heselton, Philip. *Doreen Valiente Witch.* Woodbury, MN: Llewellyn Publications, 2016.

Hohman, John George. *The Long Hidden Friend.* Edited by Gemma Gary. London: Troy Books, 2013.

Hole, Christina. *Witchcraft in England.* London: B. T. Batsford, 1947.

Horace. *The Complete Odes and Epodes.* Translated by David West. New York: Oxford University Press, 1997.

Howard, Michael. *By Moonlight and Spirit Flight.* Richmond Vista, CA: Three Hands Press, 2013.

———. *Children of Cain.* Richmond Vista: Three Hands Press, 2011.

———. *East Anglian Witches and Wizards*. Richmond Vista, CA: Three Hands Press, 2017.

———. *Modern Wicca*. Woodbury, MN: Llewellyn Publications, 2010.

———. *Scottish Witches and Warlocks*. Richmond Vista, CA: Three Hands Press, 2013.

———. *Welsh Witches and Wizards*. Richmond Vista, CA: Three Hands Press, 2009.

———. *West Country Witches*. Richmond Vista, CA: Three Hands Press, 2010.

Huson, Paul. *Mastering Herbalism*. New York: Stein and Day Publishers, 1975.

———. *Mastering Witchcraft*. New York: G. P. Putnam's Sons, 1970.

Hutton, Ronald. *Triumph of the Moon*. New York: Oxford University Press, 1999.

———. *The Witch*. New Haven, CT: Yale University Press, 2017.

Illes, Judika. *The Element Encyclopedia of Witchcraft*. London: HarperCollins Publishers, 2005.

John of Monmouth. *Genuine Witchcraft Explained*. Somerset, UK: Capall Bann Publishing, 2012.

King, Graham. *The British Book of Spells and Charms*. London: Troy Books, 2014.

Kramer, Heinrich, and Jacob Sprenger. *The Malleus Maleficarum*. 1486. Translated by Montague Summers. Mineola, NY: Dover Publications, 1971.

Le Beau, Bryan F. *The Story of the Salem Witch Trials*. New York: Routledge, 2016.

Lehner, Ernst, and Johanna Lehner. *Folklore and Symbolism of Flowers, Plants and Trees*. Mineola, NY: Dover Publications, 2003.

Leland, Charles Godfrey. *Aradia: Gospel of the Witches*. London: David Nutt, 1899. Reprint, Glastonbury, UK: The Lost Library, 2012.

Lindow, John. *Norse Mythology: A Guide to Gods, Heroes, Rituals, and Beliefs*. New York: Oxford University Press, 2001.

Lupa. *Skin Spirits*. Stafford, UK: Megalithica Books, 2009.

McNeill, F. Marian. *The Silver Bough*. Edinburgh, UK: Canongate Publishing, 1989.

Meyer, Regula. *Animal Messengers*. Rochester, VT: Bear and Company, 2015.

Mofford, Juliet Haines. *The Devil Made Me Do It!: Crime and Punishment in Early New England*. Guilford, CT: Globe Pequot Press, 2012.

Mooney, Thorn. *Traditional Wicca: A Seeker's Guide*. Woodbury, MN: Llewellyn Publications, 2018.

Moore, Arthur William. *The Folk-Lore of the Isle of Man*. London: Brown & Son, 1891. https://archive.org/details/folkloreofisleof00moor/page/n6.

Murray, Margaret. *The God of the Witches*. London: Oxford University Press, 1970.

———. *The Witch-Cult in Western Europe*. New York: Barnes and Noble, 1996.

Patterson, Steve. *Cecil Williamson's Book of Witchcraft*. London: Troy Books, 2014.

Pearson, Nigel. *The Devil's Plantation*. London: Troy Books, 2015.

———. *Treading the Mill*. London: Troy Books, 2016.

———. *Walking the Tides*, London: Troy Books, 2017.

Penczak, Christopher, editor. *Ancestors of the Craft*. Salem, NH: Copper Cauldron Publishing, 2013.

Pitcairn, Robert. *Ancient Criminal Trials in Scotland*. Vol. 3, pt. 2. Edinburgh, UK: Bannatyne Club, 1833. https://books.google.com/books?id=9td LAAAAYAAJ.

Rosen, Barbara. *Witchcraft in England, 1558–1618*. Amherst, MA: The University of Massachusetts Press, 1991.

Roth, Harold. *The Witching Herbs*. Newburyport, MA: Weiser Books, 2017.

Schulke, Daniel. *Thirteen Pathways of Occult Herbalism*. Richmond Vista, CA: Three Hands Press, 2017.

Scott, Walter. *Letters on Demonology and Witchcraft*. London: John Murray, 1830. https://catalog.hathitrust.org/Record/001024364.

Short, William R. *Icelanders in the Viking Age: The People of the Sagas*. Jefferson, NC: McFarland & Company, 2010.

Valiente, Doreen. *An ABC of Witchcraft*. Custer, WA: Phoenix Publishing, 1973.

———. *Natural Magic*, Custer, WA: Phoenix Publishing, 1986.

———. *The Rebirth of Witchcraft*. London: Robert Hale, 1989.

———. *Witchcraft for Tomorrow*. Custer, WA: Phoenix Publishing, 1978.

Westwood, Jennifer, and Sophia Kingshill. *The Lore of Scotland: A Guide to Scottish Legends*. London: Random House UK, 2009.

Wilby, Emma. *Cunning Folk and Familiar Spirits*. Brighton, UK: Sussex Academic Press, 2005.

———. *The Visions of Isobel Gowdie*, Brighton, UK: Sussex Academic Press, 2010.

Wilson, Joseph B. "Those Pesky Riddles." 1734 Witchcraft. Accessed April 30, 2019. http://www.1734-witchcraft.org/riddles.html.

Winsham, Willow. *Accused: British Witches Throughout History*. South Yorkshire, UK: Pen & Sword Books, 2016.

Zakroff, Laura Tempest. *Weave the Liminal: Living Modern Traditional Witchcraft*. Woodbury, MN: Llewellyn Publications, 2019.